Progressive Stages of Meditation on Emptiness

by

Khenpo Tsultrim Gyamtso Rinpoche

Translated and arranged by Lama Shenpen Hookham

1st edition: 1986 Longchen Foundation

2nd edition: 2001 Zhyisil Chokyi Ghatsal
3rd edition: 2016 Shrimala Trust

ISBN-13: 978-1537409009

ISBN-10: 153740900X

This edition published by the Shrimala Trust 2016

Khenpo Tsultrim Gyamtso Rinpoche

Khenpo Rinpoche is one of the foremost living teachers of the Kagyu tradition of Tibetan Buddhism, a great scholar and master of meditation who traveled the world teaching in Buddhist centres everywhere.

In his late teens and early twenties he trained as a yogin in Tibet with a local yogin known as Zopa Tharchin. He spent his early youth in retreat in the mountains until his teacher told him to study for the benefit of others. A renowned scholar, he has always excelled in philosophical debate and turned the minds of his opponents and students towards their own inner experience rather than getting lost in intellectual fabrications.

After the communist invasion of Tibet, Khenpo Rinpoche fled to India in 1960. He spent many years in Bhutan as a wandering yogin, meditating in caves and hermitages. In 1975 he was asked by the sixteenth Karmapa, head of the Kagyu tradition, to be abbot of the main Kagyu centre in France. However he asked instead to be allowed to travel and help people everywhere.

He has done that ever since, leading a truly simple, homeless life; he is a master of non-attachment. He has many times refused to accept property to build Buddhist centres and he has regularly given away all of his money. Khenpo Rinpoche has always demonstrated the carefree life of a yogin, singing spontaneous songs of realisation wherever he went, devoted only to the welfare of others.

Contents

Preface to the 2016 Edition

The Venerable Khenpo Tsultrim Gyamtso Rinpoche came to Europe at the request of H.H. 16th Karmapa in 1977. He is one of the most erudite scholars and accomplished yogins of the Karma Kagyu lineage of our day. He is especially well known for his breadth of vision and the clarity of his Dharma expositions.

While he unites prodigious scholarship with great compassion, he also embodies the training and temperament of a true yogin. In fact he is often compared to the great yogin Milarepa. Like him he is known for his spontaneous songs of realization.

For decades he travelled around the world teaching wherever he was invited leaving an indelible impression on many sanghas. At the same time in conjunction with Thrangu Rinpoche he was training the next generation of Kagyu tulkus and khenpos at the Nalanda Institute for Higher Studies in Rumtek, Sikkim. He also founded and continues to support nunneries in Tibet, Bhutan and Nepal. These are just a few of the things he has accomplished in his life. For more information go to his website - marpafoundation.org.

The Marpa Foundation, based in USA, supports his various projects including his nunneries and archives of his teachings. More recently his students have formed the Marpa Network in Europe and Asia to keep in touch with each other and work together to carry Rinpoche's vision forward. Ponlop Rinpoche, who regards Khenpo Rinpoche as his root Lama, draws on his teachings in his

Nithartha Insitute programmes (nalandabodhi.org for details).

At present Khenpo Rinpoche is in his eighties living at Tekchokling nunnery that he founded in Boudhanath, Nepal.

He first taught the progressive stages on Emptiness in Europe in 1978 and over the years he taught it again on a number of occasions in different countries, including America in 1985.

Much of his presentation derived from Jamgon Kongtrul's Encyclopaedia of Knowledge (*shes bya kun khyab*). Kongtrul was a great Kagyu teacher of the late 19th century, famous for his non-sectarian approach.

In 1979 he asked me to write a small booklet by transcribing his teachings given that year to the Kagyupa Institute of Mahayana Buddhist Studies (Kagyu Tekchen Shedra) in Brussels. Due to circumstances, which forced me to produce the booklet very hurriedly, it was inadequate in many ways. Nonetheless it was well received and immediately translated into French and Greek. Over the years that elapsed since the appearance of the first edition Khenpo Rinpoche further clarified a number of questions for me and has asked me to include the clarifications in subsequent editions. With Khenpo Rinpoche's permission I have also included a number of points that arose in the discussions my husband Michael Hookham and I had with Khenpo Rinpoche in Brussels and Oxford in 1984 and 1985.

This present edition has been further edited to remove mistakes and to clarify a number of points. Lama Tashi

Lhamo and Chryssoula Zerbini are involved in translating the text into Spanish at this time and they had various queries. Chryssoula helpfully drew my attention to points that needed clarifying and correcting. This text represents, therefore, a more refined and extensive version of the original transcribed course and earlier editions. The second edition in particular needed correcting because in some places key sentences were missing.

Since it was first published in 1986, the text has been translated into many languages right across the world and has been used in many Dharma centres and even academic institutions as a basis for courses by many teachers. This edition is currently being made into an audio-book.

Although there are recordings available from the Marpa Foundation of the original teachings Rinpoche gave on the subject of progressive stages of meditation on Emptiness, there is no recording that corresponds to this text exactly since it was put together from drawing on a number of very similar recordings and then incorporating other explanatory material into the text to help it flow more easily in English. Although there are significant changes in this edition, in the main these are small compared to the bulk of the material, which is the same in each edition.

My aim has always been to present all Rinpoche's points clearly and accurately in a readable form. To the extent that I have failed I apologize. At least I can hope that my work will inspire others to produce something better!

I should add that in some places I have included discussion of views commonly held by westerners. I found that a number of intelligent and perceptive proof-readers had difficulty in relating to the subject matter, because of certain assumptions they were making as westerners, concerning what Khenpo Tsultrim was saying. Since I find these questions often arise, I have tried to circumvent misunderstanding by actually formulating them in ways I have heard expressed and then showing how they relate to the subject matter in hand. In general, where the views of westerners are referred to, these sections represent my own additions.

Shenpen Hookham

August 2016

The Hermitage, Ynys Graianog, Criccieth LL52 0NT

Introduction

Progressive stages of meditation on Emptiness (Tib. *stong nyid sgom rim*) is a series of meditation practices on a particular aspect of the Buddha's teachings. The idea is that by beginning with one's first rather coarse common sense understanding, one progresses through increasingly subtle and more refined stages until one arrives at complete and perfect understanding. Each stage in the process prepares the mind for the next in so far as each step is fully integrated into one's understanding through the meditation process.

Three Stages in the Process of Understanding

Meditation should be understood as the third stage in the development of one's understanding. The first stage is to listen to or study the teachings with an open and receptive mind that does not distort what is being heard or studied. The second stage is carefully to reflect on what has been received in order to clarify its true significance. The third stage is to integrate the newly acquired knowledge or understanding into one's being or character. In a sense this is like putting it into practice. When one talks about meditation practice one does not mean one is practising meditation so that one day one will have perfected it and be able to give a perfect performance. Rather it is practice in the sense of actually doing or being it as opposed to just thinking about it.

Three Fields of Investigation

The whole of Buddhism is structured around this three-fold training in listening, reflecting and meditating. While Buddhist scholars concentrate on studying or listening to the Buddha's doctrine, the logicians study valid means of knowing and reasoning, the tools with which one reflects and is able to discern what is true and false. This corresponds to the stage of reflection. The yogins or meditators are those who have established through listening and reflection what must be the case and who are now engaged in training themselves in the art of abandoning their delusions. It is one thing to decide through reasoning what must be true and another actually to see the world in that way.

By relying on these three practices and using each to enhance the others, the fog of confusion and clouds of ignorance are removed; knowledge and understanding can then shine forth unimpeded, like the sun breaking through the mist at dawn.

Three Ways to Remove Doubt

At the listening stage a person should study the Buddha's word in the Sutras and commentaries, relying on explanations of qualified teachers who can clarify one's doubts.

At the reflecting stage one discovers further areas that lack clarity, and a teacher's guidance will again be required. After further reflection yet more doubts may arise so the process has to be repeated until a certitude concerning the meaning and significance of the teaching has arisen. With this certitude, or confidence, one is able to embark on meditation. Through meditation, doubts and hesitations should disappear, so if one finds them increasing one should resort once more to listening and reflecting.

As the doubts disappear, one experiences directly the true meaning of the teachings so that eventually one's meditation stabilizes free from hesitation or uncertainty.

Although people vary as to how much time they have to spend at each stage, everyone needs each stage of the process if they are to reach liberation. Meditation without listening and reflecting is blind, but listening and reflecting without meditation is like having eyesight and no legs.

Three Texts to Follow

There are Buddhist texts that correspond to each stage of this process.

For example the *Jewel Ornament of Liberation* (*dwags po thar rgyan*) by Gampopa lays out the paths and stages of the Bodhisattva according to the Mahayana Sutras. This corresponds to the listening stage where one learns about the vast and profuse aspects of the relative truth, for example karma, impermanence, love and compassion. One can practise progressive stages of meditation (*sgom rim*) on this text by reflecting systematically on its main points. Thus by studying this text one can reflect and meditate on relative truth.

The *Madhyamakavatara* (*dbu ma la 'jug pa*) by Chandrakirti gives a logical exposition of the absolute truth of emptiness. After studying this text one can reflect and meditate on Absolute Truth. This book, *Progressive Stages of Meditation on Emptiness*, is intended to assist the development of the meditator's understanding of this.

The *Mahayanaottaratantrashastra* (also known as the *Ratnagotravibhaga*, Tib. *rGyud bla ma*) is attributed in the Tibetan tradition to Maitreya. It introduces the meditator to the doctrine of Tathagatagarbha (Buddha Nature) which concerns the Clear Light Nature of Mind. It emphasizes that for the ultimate realization of Buddhahood to arise one has to experience one's true nature directly without any conceptual effort to clear away delusion or to create an Enlightened state. It teaches that as long as one does not experience the full extent of the powers of the Enlightened Mind, one has not reached complete liberation. This is a more subtle teaching than merely that of showing all *dharmas* are empty of self-nature. It should be studied and practised after the progressive meditation on emptiness that is outlined in this book.

The doctrine of *Tathagatagarbha* outlined in the Mahayanao*ttaratantrashastra* lays the basis for understanding Vajrayana and Mahamudra teachings and practice. These teachings take for granted that practitioners have already understood the vast aspects of the relative truth, and the empty nature of all *dharmas*, so that they are ready to relax in the Clear Light Nature of Mind just as it is, here and now, using all experience to enhance the clarity of his understanding.

The Importance of the Relative Truth (Skt. *Samvrtisatya,* Tib. *kun rdzob bden pa*)

From these explanations it will be clear that as a preliminary to following the 'Progressive stages of Meditation on Emptiness' one should listen to, reflect on and meditate on the 'Jewel Ornament of Liberation' or some similar text.

Without a proper understanding of the vast aspects of the relative truth, meditation on Emptiness can be misleading and even dangerous.

Although insight may come quickly, stability comes slowly. The relative truth gives us a way of looking at life and the world which, while conforming to our ordinary common sense notions of time and space, is conducive to Enlightenment (i.e. Liberation) which lies beyond them.

The relative truth is the foundation of all the Buddha's teaching because it gives a proper understanding of what is to be abandoned and what is to be cultivated. By abandoning unwholesome and cultivating wholesome action, one creates the necessary conditions for listening, reflecting and meditating to be fruitful. In this way it is through respecting the relative truth that the Absolute truth can be realized.

Absolute Truth (Skt. *Paramarthasatya,* Tib. *don dam bden pa)*

In Buddhism, Absolute Truth or Absolute Reality means the end point of one's analysis, in other words, the most basic or fundamental element of existence or experience.

For example, if one takes a clay pot, a potter might say that in absolute terms it was clay, but a scientist might say it was a collection of atoms. If he were being more precise he might say the atoms themselves consisted of atomic particles moving in space, but even this would be a rough approximation to reality. In absolute terms atomic particles can no longer be defined precisely these days. They cannot be said to be this or that or here or there; they have to be expressed in terms of probability. No doubt scientists will express it differently again in a few years' time.

In the same way Absolute Truth presents itself differently to practitioners at the various levels of their practice. Just as this emerges in the experience of an individual practitioner, it occurs historically in the way that the Buddhist Scriptures emerged as a progression of increasingly subtle teachings.

Progressive Stages of Meditation on Emptiness

This book *Progressive Stages of Meditation on Emptiness* presents the key stages in the Buddhist experience of the Absolute Truth of Emptiness as five-fold:

1. the Shravaka stage,

2. the Chittamatra stage,

3. the Svatantrika-Madhyamaka stage,

4. the Prasangika-Madhyamaka stage.

5. the Shentong or Great Madhyamaka stage.

Although these stages are named after the Buddhist Schools that formulated them, in fact, they represent the stages in the development of an individual's understanding of emptiness.

We are not interested at this point in getting involved in scholastic and philosophical debate about exactly how each school worked out its system in detail. The point is that these stages represent five readily recognizable stages in the progression from a gross cognisance to increasingly subtle levels of understanding.

In general, practitioners should be given teachings that correspond with their capacities and level of understanding. However, except for the occasional well-endowed practitioner, most people cannot understand and practise the most subtle and profound teachings on emptiness as soon as they hear them. Instead, they have to progress through a series of levels starting with the most basic teaching, just as one has to start in class one at school and gradually work one's way up from there.

For example, in the case of a very technical subject, one does not expect to understand the subtleties discussed by experts without having learnt the first principles. In the same way it is highly unlikely that a person will gain an accurate understanding of the most profound teachings of the Buddha without having gone through the progressive stages of the teaching leading up to them.

One can think of the progressive stages of meditation on Emptiness as the stages in the refinement process of a piece of gold ore. The initial stages of the process are somewhat gross but nonetheless effective, the later stages become more and more refined until finally the completely pure refined gold itself emerges. Here the gold is compared to the Absolute Truth of the Emptiness itself.

Another example of how the stages of the meditation represent a progression from gross to subtle is that of a person being instructed on how to find a needle on a mountain. First he needs to know the general direction of the mountain for which he needs a large scale map. Once he has found the mountain he needs a small scale map in order to find the exact location. It may lie near a large rock for example. On nearing the rock he can be shown the exact tree under which it lies. On arriving under the tree he needs the exact place pointed out. Finally, however, it is with his own eyes that he has to find it. In the same way the early stages of the meditation progression bring one nearer and nearer to the true realization of Emptiness, but finally it is through one's own direct perception that it is seen.

Stage One: Shravaka Meditation on Not-Self

Although this is called the Shravaka stage because it represents the heart of the Shravaka vehicle, one should not assume that it is unimportant in the other vehicles of Buddhism. Milarepa, the great Vajrayana master, taught his disciple, the shepherd boy, the Shravaka meditation on not-self after the boy had shown signs of having great natural meditation ability. It is said that on being told to meditate on a small image of the Buddha he went straight into meditative absorption (*samadhi*) for a week without noticing the time. When he came out of *samadhi* it seemed to him he had only been meditating a few seconds.

At this stage one does not consider the emptiness of all phenomena, but only the emptiness or not-self of the person. The importance of this is that it is the clinging to a false idea of a permanent, single and independent self that is the root cause of all one's suffering. One does not need to have an explicit or clearly formulated idea of such a self in order to act as if one had one. 'Self' here means the implied self, which might also be regarded as implied in the behaviour of animals. Animals, just like us, identify themselves with their bodies and minds and are constantly seeking physical and mental comfort as they try to avoid discomfort and assuage pain. Both animals and humans act as if they had a self to protect and preserve and one regards this behaviour as automatic and instinctive as well as normal. When pain or discomfort arise, the automatic response is to try to remove it. It is extraneous to the self and the implication is that the self would naturally be happy if all pain and suffering were removed.

Strangely, however, when we try to analyse our behaviour in relation to this self, we realize that we are very unclear as to what this self really is. Non-Buddhist thinkers have defined the self variously as resting in the brain, blood or heart and having such qualities as true or transcendental existence in or outside of the mind or body. To have any meaning such a self has to be lasting, for if it perished every moment one would not be so concerned about what was going to happen to it the next moment; it would not be one's 'self' anymore. Again it has to be single. If one had no individual, separate identity why should one worry about what happened to one's 'self' any more than one worried about anyone else's. It has to be independent or there would be no sense in saying 'I did this' or 'I have that'. If one had no independent existence there would be no-one to claim the actions and experiences as its own.

We all act as if we had permanent, single and independent selves that it is our constant pre-occupation to protect and foster. It is an unthinking habit that most of us would normally be most unlikely to question or explain. However, all our suffering is associated with this pre-occupation. All loss and gain, pleasure and pain arise because we identify so closely with this vague feeling of self-ness that we have. We are so emotionally involved with and attached to this 'self' that we take it for granted.

Meditators do not speculate about this 'self'. They do not have theories about whether it does or does not exist. Instead they just train themselves to watch dispassionately how their mind clings to the idea of self and mine and how all their sufferings arise from this attachment. At the same time they look carefully for that self. They try to isolate it from all their other experiences. Since it is the culprit as far as all their suffering is concerned, they want to find it and identify it. The irony is that however much they try, they do not find anything that corresponds to this self.

Westerners often confuse self in this context with person, ego or personality. They argue that they do not think of the person, ego or personality as a permanent, single and independent entity. This is to miss the point. The person, personality, or ego as such, are not a problem. One can analyse them quite rationally into their constituent parts. The Western tradition has all sorts of ways of doing this. The Buddhist way is to talk of the five *skandhas*, the eighteen *dhatus* or the twelve gates of consciousness. The question is not whether or not the person, personality or ego is a changing, composite train of events conditioned by many complex factors. Any rational analysis shows us that this is the case. The question is why then do we behave emotionally as if it were permanent, single and independent. Thus, when looking for the self it is very important to remember it is an emotional response that one is examining. When one responds to events as if one had a self, for example when one feels very hurt or offended, one should ask oneself who or what exactly is feeling hurt or offended.

If you are not convinced that you behave emotionally as if you had a lasting, single and independent self, then it is important to address yourself to this issue before moving on to consider the doctrine of not-self. Think carefully about pain and suffering and ask yourself who or what it is that is suffering. Who is afraid of what will happen; who feels bad about what has happened; why does death seem such a threat when the present disappears every moment, scarcely having had a chance to arise? You will find that your thinking is full of contradictions, inconsistencies and irresolvable paradoxes. This is normal. Everyone (except, perhaps, the insane) have a common sense notion of what or who they are which works (more or less) and enables them to function as normal human beings.

However, when meditators address themselves to what or who this self is, they cannot find it. Then gradually, very gradually, it dawns on them that the reason they cannot find it is that it is not there and never was. There is tremendous emotional resistance to this realization so it takes a long time to break through, but when it does there is an immediate release of tension and suffering. The cause of it has gone. The cause of it was a mental attachment to something that was not there.

Sometimes the resistance to the realization takes the form of irritation. One is used to being able to explain things to oneself rationally. Experience of the self is so direct and in a sense so obvious, there seems to be no reason to include it in one's rational explanation of things. On the other hand, when one does try to explain it to oneself, the whole thing is so irritatingly subjective it seems one could never reach any satisfactory conclusion. Instead of letting the mind rest in the actual experience of that paradox, one gets frustrated and irritated at not being able to form a water-tight explanation of what the self is. It is important to notice that and be aware of it. If one tries to just push that irritation out of one's mind, one will never have a deep realization of not-self.

Clinging to the idea of self is like clinging to the idea that a piece of rope in the dark is a snake. When the light is turned on and one sees that there is no snake there, one's fear and suffering that arose from clinging to it as real dissolve. The snake never existed in the first place, so it was simply one's clinging to that idea that caused the suffering and nothing else. The wisdom that realizes not-self is like the light that revealed the rope was not a snake.

Clearly, in order to end one's own suffering, there is nothing more important than to realize that when one takes the body and mind to be a permanent, single and independent self, one unthinkingly attributes to them qualities which they simply do not have. Nothing in the whole stream of mental and physical phenomena that constitute one's experience of body and mind has the quality of permanent, unitary and independent existence. It is all changing and impermanent, moment by moment. One's persistent effort to treat it as if it were the self, makes it a constant stream of suffering (*duhkha*).

Realizing not-self is the first step to realizing the empty nature of all phenomena. That is why the first teachings of the Buddha concern the Three Marks of Existence i.e. suffering, impermanence, and not-self.

The Dream Example

The Buddha often used the example of a dream to illustrate his teachings on emptiness and this example can be applied with increasing subtlety at each stage of the meditation progression on Emptiness. It is a good example for showing how the two truths, relative and absolute, work together. In a dream there is a sense of being a person with a body and mind living in a world of things to which one feels attracted or averse depending on how they appear. As long as one does not realize it is just a dream, one takes all these things as real and one feels happy or sad on account of them.

For example, one may dream of being eaten by a tiger or being burnt in a fire. In the absolute truth no-one is being eaten or burnt, but still in terms of the dream one might really suffer as if one had been. The suffering arises simply by virtue of the fact that one identifies oneself with the person in the dream. As soon as one becomes aware that it is only a dream, even if the dream does not stop, one is nonetheless free to think, 'It does not matter; it is only a dream. It is not really happening to me.' The person that was suffering in the dream only arose as a temporary manifestation dependent on the condition of one's not being aware that it was only a dream. It had no permanent, unitary and independent self of its own.

Understanding this intellectually is not enough to free oneself from the strongly ingrained habit of clinging to one's mind and body as a permanent, single and independent self. One has to examine the stream of one's mental and physical experience again and again, reflecting on what one does or does not find until one reaches total conviction and certainty. Having become convinced of what is the case, one then has to meditate, resting the mind in this new-found knowledge until the veils caused by one's habitual patterns of thought have finally dissolved. At this point direct, unmistakable realization of not-self arises and it is this genuine experience that actually liberates one from suffering.

Method of Investigation

Instinctively we identify ourselves with our bodies and minds. We have a very strong emotional attachment to them even though our whole idea of self and mine is very vague and confused. For example, when we are sick we sometimes say, 'I am sick', and yet in the very next breath we may say, '...because I have a headache'. What do we mean? Do we mean the I is one thing and the head another? Or do we mean that the head is the I? One should begin one's investigation with these very common sense notions of 'I' and 'I, the doer' or 'I, the experiencer'.

One could think for example of having one's limbs and organs removed or transplanted. If one were given another man's heart would it really affect the 'I'? We naturally think that 'I' (the experiencer or doer) has now received a new heart. One does not think that one is grafting a new heart into the 'I' as such. How far can one go with this process? With limbs and organs it seems quite clear that the 'I' is a separate entity, but what about the brain? Suppose one had another man's brain implanted into one's skull. Would that affect the 'I'? One might find oneself wondering whether 'I' (the experiencer or doer) could actually use another man's brain and yet still be the same person. One might wonder if one might find some actions governed by the 'I' one has now and some actions governed by the 'I' of the person from whom the brain was taken. Of course one cannot know what the result of such a transplant would be, were it ever possible to perform it, but instinctively one feels it is important to know whether the 'I' would be affected or not.

Although this seems so important, we are still very unclear about what this 'I' might be. We may wonder if it is, perhaps, just a small vital part of the brain. However, when one thinks about it, one is not emotionally attached to a minute mechanism in one's grey matter. If that were all one's emotional attachment were about, it would be easy enough to remove and all the suffering with it. Life would not need to have any meaning, nor human life any particular value. There would be no need to go on struggling in a life full of suffering and frustration. However, such a view strikes us as totally nihilistic and demeaning. The 'I' feels it is more important than that.

The 'I' that we are emotionally attached to seems to step back and look on life, evaluating experience and wishing to avoid suffering. We do not experience it or treat it the way we would a physical object like a brain. We know from general knowledge gleaned from other people that the brain is in the skull. It can be physically located, touched and measured. It has some relationship with the mind because, when our mental state changes, a change can often be detected in the brain. However, whatever scientists may find out about the brain, they will only be able to tell us the relationship between mind and brain in more detail. They can look, probe and measure to find facts about what the brain is doing, but how will they know what the mind is experiencing as they do it? They may, for example, be able to say there is a lot of activity in such and such region of the brain when a person thinks of red. But how do they know the person is really experiencing red? The person himself knows for sure the nature of his experience. He may call it red. He may not. He may not call it anything. He will never know if anyone else ever experiences anything in the way that he does, even if everyone agrees to call the experience they have by the same name. Who can know how anything is experienced other than the experiencer? A scientist can say the brain is acting as if it were experiencing red because the brain is doing what it always does when people are experiencing red. Who will know if they are right in any particular case or not? Only the experiencer can know for sure. The scientist relies on well-informed guess-work. Certain theories are taken to be true because they seem to explain events very well.

The main thrust of Buddhism, however, is not about theories at all. It is about experience. In particular it is concerned with the experience of suffering. What

Buddhism has discovered is that the experience of suffering is always associated with strong emotional attachment to a vague sense of 'self'. So Buddhism turns its attention onto that strong emotional response associated with that sense of 'self' and asks about how that self is actually experienced. Where is that 'I' experienced?

One might answer that one experiences it in the brain. However, one does not need to know anything about the brain in order to suffer. Even a dog or a child suffers. They do not have theories about the self, but their behaviour suggests that they are attached to a sense of self. If they were not, why would a child or a dog existing in one instant of time concern itself about a dog or a child that was going to exist in the next moment? Surely it is because unconsciously he is thinking that the dog or the child of the next moment is still 'him' in some sense and is distinct from anyone else. When he sees a threat to his life or comfort he recoils from it. Unconsciously he is thinking that 'he' could escape this threat and continue his existence somewhere more pleasant; this shows he has a sense of having an independent existence.

One could argue that in lower forms of living organisms recoiling from unpleasant stimuli is simply a mechanical response, like trees waving in the wind. Maybe that is true for primitive forms of life, but this does not have any bearing on the problem of suffering at all. If we were merely complex mechanical devices one could argue that objectively suffering did not matter. This would be an extremely impoverished attitude to life and not a very convincing one.

One may feel that what one really means when one says that suffering is experienced in the brain is that it is experienced in the mind. Since, in modern western society one automatically assumes that the mind is in the brain, and since one's notion of mind is so vague anyway, there does not seem to be much difference between talking about the mind and talking about the brain. However, they cannot be synonymous, even if ultimately they are discovered to be of the same stuff, or nature.

One cannot avoid the question of what we mean by mind. We are extremely vague and imprecise in our everyday, common-sense way of talking about it. Sometimes it seems we identify ourselves with our mind, as for example when we say we are happy or sad. Although we mean the mind is happy or sad, we do not really make a distinction between our self and our mind. Nevertheless, we also find ourselves saying things like, 'I could not control my mind'. Incidentally, we also say, 'I could not control myself', as if one had two selves. This seems to be the same lack of clarity that enables us sometimes to talk as if the self were the mind and sometimes as if the self owned the mind.

One might be tempted at this point to start speculating about the nature of the mind and the self. One might even wax philosophical about it, reflecting on such statements as, 'I think, therefore I am'. However, since 'I am' is merely a thought, the only thing we are really sure of is the experience of thought. So the only sure means of finding out what that experience is, is to experience it as precisely and as dispassionately as is possible. So the Shravaka approach is to investigate experience by simply being as aware as possible every moment.

In order to carry out this investigation as systematically as possible Buddhist teachers have organized experience into a number of comprehensive sets of categories. One of these sets of categories is called the five *skandhas*, which literally means the five heaps. They are called heaps because, looked at dispassionately, all our experience arises moment by moment as isolated, impersonal events. After they have arisen, so soon after that it seems simultaneous, we become emotionally involved and create a whole scenario of 'self' versus 'world' or 'other'.

The five *skandhas* are form, feeling, perception, mental constructions and consciousness.

Form

Form refers to the body and the environment. We take for granted that there is a world 'out there' beyond our senses and that our body partakes of that world. When we sit down to meditate it is the body and its environment that first catch our attention. So we can start our investigation there. I am sitting here because my body is sitting here. Is that 'I' therefore the body?

One can examine the body systematically taking it limb by limb, organ by organ. Is my hand me? Am I still me without my hand?

What is a hand anyway? Is it still a hand without fingers? Without skin? Without bone? Without flesh? When it is broken down in this way one finds that 'hand' is merely a convenient concept. There is no such thing as a 'hand' as such. It is the same for every part of the body. It is the same right down to the tiniest cell, and the tiniest atom and the tiniest part of an atom as scientists know only too well. However far one investigates one will always find more parts and as each part is given a name, each part will be found to break up into something other than itself. The process is endless.

Examining the body in this way one may come to the conclusion that 'I' and 'body' are merely convenient concepts for dealing with the world and experience. They have a certain relative reality, but they are not absolutes. In the relative truth they are streams of events that one identifies and labels as 'I' or 'body'. But that 'I' or 'body' cannot be said to have permanent, unitary and independent existence. If the body had such existence it might have been called the self, but it does not have, and however much one were to investigate it, it never would have. It is not-self and self is not the body. The same applies for the brain of course.

Feeling

Feeling here refers specifically to those of pleasure, displeasure and indifference. For example, as one sits in meditation, one may like it and want to stay, or one may not and want to leave. The only other alternative is that one may not care one way or the other. Wherever we are and whatever we are doing, we are always experiencing one or other of these three feelings. They are not-self, however, because none of them is lasting; they take turns in arising; now there is happiness, now sadness and so on. Self could not be the feelings because they are always changing.

Perception

Perception here refers to the first moment of recognition of input through the senses. When one experiences a colour such as blue one recognizes it as blue, when one feels an itch one recognizes the feeling, or when one hears a car starting up one recognizes the sound, and the same applies to smells etc. We experience a continual stream of perceptions through our senses all the time we are awake. We are either listening to something, looking at something, feeling something with our sense of touch, tasting or smelling something or even receiving the image of something arising in the mind. We have six senses including the mind. As one sits in meditation one might be perceiving the breath moving in and out, images floating into the mind, or noises going on in the street outside and so on. Although one thinks it is one's self that is perceiving these things one does not think these perceptions are the self. None of them has the characteristics of self since none of them is lasting.

Mental Constructions

Mental constructions include all the mental activity of thinking, patterns of thought, negative emotions such as desire, pride, and jealousy, and healthy emotions such as love, devotion and patience. In fact feelings and perceptions are mental constructions too, but for the sake of this categorization they are here listed separately. The term in Sanskrit for this heap (*skandha*) is *samskara* (Tib. *'du byed*). *Samskara* also has the meaning of predisposition in the sense of tracks left by former deeds that condition one's present thinking and behaviour. The Tibetan term *'dus byed* is a general term meaning mental constructions of any kind. Although we should understand that everything that arises in the mind is conditioned by what has gone before, in general we can just take this *skandha* to mean all mental events not included in the other three mental *skandhas*.

Although we do not think of mental constructions or mental events as being self, we do tend to identify our self with what we conceive to be our personality. Emotionally, if some part of our personality is criticized, we feel we (our self) has been criticized. However, if one examines the make-up of one's personality very carefully and dispassionately one finds it even more intangible than the body. At least with the body one was sure what was included as part of it, even though none of it could be identified as the self. With one's personality, on the other hand, one just has a stream of ever changing mental constructions and events. One tends to choose certain, more or less constant features of this stream as characteristic of a particular personality, and when they manifest one feels a person is being himself. If he starts to manifest (again in a more or less constant fashion) totally different characteristics from before, we talk about him having had a change of personality. We talk of people not being in their right mind, of being temporarily deranged and so on. The implication is that there is a person or self other than the present personality or mind state. It is this self that we are investigating. It is clearly not the personality or any of the mental constructions or events that constitute it, since none of them exhibits a permanent, unitary and independent element that one could call the self.

Consciousness

A consciousness in Buddhism refers to a moment of awareness. As we think about the four *skandhas* that have already been listed we might feel that behind all of them was a general sense of awareness or knowing. We might even call it the mind itself as opposed to the mental events that occur within it. We might feel that this is really what we mean by the 'I' or the self. It seems to be an unchanging, unitary, independent awareness that is just going on as the basis of all our experience and it is this awareness that is 'I', the doer. Let's examine this idea carefully.

Generally speaking, we think of our life and experience going along as a sort of stream in time and space. There is a sense of beginning and end and one event following on from another. Even though one does not think exactly in terms of a moment of experience having edges round it, nevertheless there is a sense of its ending somewhere, otherwise it would just merge into everything else. So our experience and our sense of self is definitely bounded by time and space. Therefore, it must be possible to divide it up into the smallest conceivable parts and the smallest conceivable moments of time. In the Shravaka approach one tries to be aware of the smallest conceivable moments of experience in order to be sure that one has missed nothing in one's search for a lasting, unitary, permanent self.

What one finds is that every moment of experience has two aspects. If it did not have these two aspects it could hardly be counted as being a moment of experience at all. What are these two aspects? There has to be something to experience and something to experience it. In other words there is always something knowing something or being aware of something. If either of these elements were missing there would be no experience. These smallest conceivable moments of consciousness arising dependent on their corresponding momentary object of consciousness are what in Buddhism are known as consciousnesses. The term is *vijnana* (Tib. *rnam shes*). The 'vi' part of the word can mean partial or divided. Thus, a consciousness is a partial or divided knowing. This contrasts with *jnana* (Tib. *ye shes*) which means simply knowing or wisdom. The difference between *jnana* and *vijnana* becomes very important in the later stages of the progression of meditation on emptiness.

The upshot of this rather long discussion on what is meant by consciousness in Buddhism is that when, in the hopes of resolving one's difficulties, one suggests that the self is that continuing awareness that is behind all one's experience, one must in fact be referring to the stream of *vijnanas*. One may not have analysed it as deeply as that, but if one still accepts common-sense notions of time and space, then the nature of consciousness must be divisible in the way outlined above. Furthermore, since each moment of consciousness has a different object each moment of consciousness is separate and distinct. It might be a consciousness of form, sound, smell, taste, touch or mental image, but whichever it is, it is quite distinct from any other moment that has arisen before or is about to arise after it. The moment before has gone and the moment to come does not exist yet. So consciousness can only ever be momentary and such a momentary phenomenon would never qualify for the title of 'self'. Thus, the mind or awareness that seems to be behind all our experience cannot be the self either.

At the end of our analysis we arrive at the conclusion that the self is simply a vague and convenient concept that we project now here and now there onto a stream of experiences. One may wish to maintain that the self is the continuity of the stream of physical and mental events that constitute a personality and that as such it does not have to have the characteristics of being lasting, single and independent. This is simply a redefinition of the term self, but it does not explain our emotional behaviour at all. Buddhism is not telling people that they should believe that they have a self or that they do not have a self. It is saying that when one looks at the way one suffers and the way one thinks and responds emotionally to life, it is as if one believed there were a self associated with the *skandhas* that was permanent, single and independent, yet on closer analysis no such self can be isolated or found. In other words the *skandhas* are empty of a self.

In terms of relative reality, however, because one is so emotionally attached to one's concept of self, all one's mental patterning and habits of thought (*samskaras*) feed and strengthen the idea. Furthermore, the actions that one performs in the belief that it is this self acting, serve to create the 'world' that one finds oneself in. In other words, although one can find no such self in absolute terms, in terms of the relative one still has to suffer the results of one's past good and bad actions.

To illustrate this point, take, for example, a candle flame. One can, in a general way, say something like, 'That flame has been burning all day.' However, in absolute terms, no flame has been burning all day. The flame was never the same flame from one moment to the next. There was no single, independent, lasting flame there at all. What we grasp at as a flame is not there, nevertheless it is still meaningful to talk about flames.

When one meditates on the emptiness of the *skandhas,* one simply sees them as they are; they are not a permanent, single and independent self and there is no such self in them. Just as in a dream, once one sees that the person in the dream is not really oneself, any suffering that one may have felt on account of, for example, being burnt or chased by a tiger, simply fades away. In the same way, when one focuses one's attention inwardly on the absence of self in the *skandhas*, all the suffering caused by taking the *skandhas* to be the self fades away.

Then the mind can rest peacefully in empty space, with perfect confidence and assurance. Through meditation in this manner all subtle doubts are worn away and the mind can rest naturally in emptiness.

The Fruit of the Shravaka Practice

Our instinctive, emotional attachment or clinging to a vague notion of self is the source of all our suffering. From the idea of self comes that of 'other'. It is from clinging to self that the idea of other arises and desire, hatred and delusion arise. There are many kinds of desire including greed, envy and miserliness. Hatred can take the form of jealousy, anger and resentment. Delusion includes mental dullness, stupidity and confusion. From these unhealthy mental states arise actions motivated by them, and their results. The results take the form of all kinds of suffering, which one cannot escape as long as one clings to the *skandhas* as if they were the self.

Thus, the only way to remove one's suffering is to realize the *skandhas* are not-self. The wisdom (*prajna*) that realizes not-self is like light removing darkness. Just as darkness cannot exist in the light, so suffering cannot exist in the light of wisdom.

Where there is suffering, clinging to self must also be present. Where there is clinging to self, ignorance of not-self must be present. The only way to remove suffering is therefore to remove the ignorance that causes the clinging to self.

Thus the goal for the Shravaka is the removal of suffering. That goal is called nirvana. The Shravaka is not trying to remove the suffering of all beings, nor is he trying to attain Buddhahood. He does not have the vision, the understanding, nor the confidence necessary to do that. His aim is relatively modest. It is simply to remove the cause of his own suffering. Nonetheless, one cannot say that his realization of emptiness is not very profound. It is said that it corresponds to that of Bodhisattvas on the first to the sixth levels. It removes the veils of ignorance and confusion that make deeper and more subtle levels of emptiness so inaccessible. Therefore, by realizing the not-self emptiness of the *skandhas* one is preparing the way for the higher vehicles, whose goal is not just the removing of one's own suffering, but the suffering of all beings.

Meditation Procedure

Although when the progressive stages of meditation on Emptiness are being taught one often has little time to meditate on one stage before one is introduced to the next, it is best to take each stage at a time and to practise it until some definite experience has arisen.

It is important to have a regular meditation schedule, beginning with periods of 15-30 minutes in the morning and evening. One can build up from there meditating for longer and longer periods. As with study and reflection a certain amount of perseverance and effort are needed at first, but one should never let one's mind get too tight. Remember the example of the musician tuning the strings of his instrument. The tension has to be just right, neither too tight nor too loose.

Choose a definite time in the morning and evening to sit in meditation. Sit in a good meditation posture and always begin by taking refuge and rousing *Bodhichitta* motivation to gain Enlightenment for the benefit of all beings.

When you first begin the practice, reflect for some time on the meaning of not-self, and investigate in the manner explained above. However, once you have developed some confidence and understanding, do not bother to keep investigating, just go straight into the emptiness meditation. To keep returning to the investigatory stage after confidence has arisen is like keeping switching a light on and off without any purpose. Once the light is on, leave it on. When you reach the real meditation stage of your practice there will be no more need for reflection. You should just rest in the meditation without any hesitation.

At the end of each session dedicate all the merit to the Enlightenment of all beings. Between sessions reflect again and again on how there is no self in the *skandhas* and think of everything as being like a dream, a film or a magical illusion. What is appearing as a self is not your self really. Thinking like this, how can unhealthy emotions such as greed, hate and delusion arise? If these do not arise, how can suffering arise?

Stage Two: Chittamatra Mind Only

While the Shravaka stage belongs to what is sometimes called the Hinayana, the Chittamatra stage belongs to the Mahayana. Mahayana means the Great Vehicle because its goal is the great goal of the Enlightenment of all beings. This contrasts with the goal of the Hinayana which is simply the cessation of one's own personal suffering. From the Mahayana point of view, the Hinayana is a true and valid means for removing the self-clinging that gives rise to the unhealthy emotions (*klesha*), the root of all suffering. The Mahayana also accepts that the Hinayana removes the veils of ignorance that prevent one realizing the true nature of the *skandhas* as not-self, in other words as empty. However, the Mahayana teaches that Hinayana does not remove ignorance completely. It simply removes the gross ignorance that causes *kleshas* and suffering. Technically it is said to remove simply the *klesha* veils, leaving the more subtle veils called knowledge veils. *Kleshas* and suffering are extinguished like the flame of a candle whose wax is exhausted and the meditator passes into a state of peace. The meditator believes this to be nirvana.

However, the Mahayanist realizes that even in this state of peace there is still a subtle kind of ignorance. It is ignorance of the true nature of reality and this ignorance obscures the fullness of the potential that a human being has. Human beings can actually reach a state of perfect and complete Awakening in which they are endowed with all the powers of a Buddha. This means all the powers that work for the benefit of all sentient creatures and bring them finally to perfect and complete Awakening.

Thus, the motive for progressing further is compassion for other beings and the wish to remove their suffering. Compassion alone is not enough, however; it is also necessary to have the vision to see that the power to liberate others arises from seeing the true nature of reality more deeply. One has to aspire to remove all one's subtle veils of ignorance and to realize the supreme Awakening of the Buddha. These veils of ignorance are called the veils of knowledge and, though subtle, are very powerful. They pervade and distort the way one sees and understands the whole of one's experience and prevent one knowing anything properly in an absolute sense.

Thus, the Bodhisattva has two great aspirations: one is to liberate all sentient beings and the other is to realize the profound Emptiness of all phenomena, the realization of the fully Awakened Buddha. This double aspiration is called the giving rise to the Enlightened Mind (*Bodhichittotpada, byang chub sems bskyed*).

With this aspiration as the foundation, one proceeds to the next stage of the meditation on emptiness.

Chittamatra means 'mind only' or 'merely mind'. As at the Shravaka stage, at the Chittamatra stage one thinks of one's mind as a stream of moments of consciousness (*vijnana*) with a knowing and a known aspect to each moment. However, whereas at the Shravaka stage one takes for granted a world 'out there' beyond the senses, at the Chittamatra stage this is questioned. Chittamatrins do not take a sort of solipsistic view that the world is nothing but one's own invention, as if the *skandhas* were one's self. This would be like some kind of madness. As we have already seen in the Shravaka view, the Buddha taught that the *skandhas* are not self.

Essentially the Chittamatrin approach, like any Buddhist approach, is based on direct experience. Following the Shravaka pattern of trying to be intimately aware of every moment of consciousness as it arises, at the Chittamatrin stage the meditator realizes that the division of each moment of awareness into an inner perceiving mind and a separate outer perceived object is a conceptual invention. In a dream one experiences, moment by moment, inner perceiving moments of consciousness aware of seemingly outer perceived objects and yet, when one wakes up, one realizes there were no outer perceived objects other than the mind itself. Both the inner perceiving moments of consciousness and the outer perceived objects were different manifestations of mind. This shows that the mere appearance of seemingly outer perceived objects is no proof that such things exist in absolute terms. In fact, there is no proof that there is any substance other than mind anywhere. Furthermore, the Buddha Himself taught, 'The three realms of existence are merely mind'.

Thus, having already established that there is no personal self in the *skandhas*, the Chittamatrin now looks at the *skandhas* themselves with greater precision. Not only is there no permanent, single and independent self in the skandhas, but there is no difference in nature between mind and matter. Mind and matter are empty of separate, independent natures. Thus, in absolute terms, each moment of experience is empty of a difference in nature of perceiver and perceived. Rather than regarding the mind as merely the seeing or observing aspect of a moment of experience, it is also the content of that experience.

Mind is, at one and the same time, both real and empty. It is real in the sense that all experience is basically a manifestation of mind. It is empty in the sense that it is not a permanent, single, independent entity. It is instead a stream of fleeting, dependently arising moments of consciousness. Furthermore, all phenomena pertain either to the inner perceiving aspect of consciousness or to the outer perceived aspect of consciousness; in other words they are all mind. So the whole of existence is empty of a duality of substance between mind and matter. This means there is no limit to the mind or it's power. So in principle a person could realize the full powers of the Buddha's Enlightenment and work for the liberation of all beings.

On reflection, one can see that the Shravaka approach is similar to removing suffering in a dream by recognizing that the person in the dream is not really oneself. The Chittamatra approach is like removing the suffering by realizing that both the cause of the suffering, for example the fire or the tiger, and the person suffering are both nothing more than the play of the mind. Realizing that, one realizes that the fire or the tiger and the one suffering are empty of any reality of their own. Furthermore, recognizing that it is the mind producing both, one could choose to dream of whatever one wanted to. Not only is one liberated from the illusion of self, one is liberated from the sense of powerlessness. That sense of powerlessness prevents one realizing one's true nature and limits one's capacity for compassionate action.

It is important not to take the Chittamatra view to be a kind of solipsism. Chittamatra is not saying everything is oneself or one's own personal experience. There is a world that one shares with others. What Chittamatra is saying, however, is that it is not of a different substance to mind. This doctrine is very useful when discussing how a consciousness which is of a mental nature can perceive matter. There is a discontinuity between our experience and what we conceive of as the material world. For example, we experience obstruction and conceive of solidity. We never really experience solidity as such. Solidity can only be imagined by the mind. Solid, material things cannot get into the mind and float about in it. Mind cannot put out a kind of feeler into the material world and experience it. The mind simply experiences mental events and interprets them to mean there is such a thing as a material world which it then proceeds to imagine.

Quite a lot of modern scientists and philosophers think that the mind/matter dichotomy can be resolved by saying that mind is none other than matter. The interesting thing about that theory is that not only does one interpret one's experience to mean that there is a material world beyond the senses, but that that material world can produce and experience thoughts, emotions and mental images in just the same way that one's own mind does. Furthermore, these thoughts, feelings and images pertain to the material world. One is left wondering what 'material' might mean in this context.

The Dream Example

The dream example is the best means one has for understanding the Chittamatra stage of realizing Emptiness. In order to appreciate how pertinent this example is, ask yourself how you know that you are not dreaming right now?

Maybe you feel like saying, 'Because dreams are never so vivid as this, colours are not so bright, forms, sounds, smells, touch and tastes are not so clear and precise'. However, someone else might disagree and say his dreams were even more vivid than his day-time experiences. Does this then make his dreams waking experience and his waking a dream? Does it mean if your faculties become impaired so that you no longer experience things so clearly and precisely, that your life becomes a dream?

On further reflection you might suggest that you know that you are not dreaming because of the continuity of your life. Everything is in predictable places, there is a sense of cause and effect, regularity, an established pattern of events and so on. You might say that dreams are not like that. They are unpredictable; they can change in bizarre ways without warning and for no apparent reason. There is no real continuity and you might find yourself in any place, time, shape or form.

Are you saying then, that if a dream were to stabilize so that there were a continuity and a fairly predictable pattern of events, if then it were to continue for long periods of time and your waking experiences were only to last for brief periods in which you were very confused and disorientated, then the dream would have become waking experience and the waking experience a dream? For after all, it is not unusual for people to dream of ordinary situations, e.g. that they have got up and had their breakfast and gone to work and so on.

You may laugh at the suggestion that you are dreaming now. You may think that if you were asleep and dreaming everybody would stop interacting with you. They would tell you when you woke up that you had been dreaming, so there is no way that one could confuse dreaming with waking. However, there is no inherent reason why you should not dream that people have woken you up and told you that you have just awakened from a dream.

Finally one might conclude that there is no characteristic of waking experience that clearly distinguishes it from dreaming. It is only a matter of degree and of one's emotional predisposition. You believe you are awake because you want to feel secure and feel that the world is solid, real and supportive around you. If you were to seriously doubt you were awake, you would feel frightened and confused. The stability of the experience of being awake reassures you, so you believe in it and give it a reality that you do not afford to dreams. If you suffer in a dream you are happy to let it go when it ends, feeling reassured that it was not real anyway. If you suffer in what you call your waking life, you get emotionally involved in it and afford it the status of absolute reality.

Chittamatrins explain the phenomena of dreaming as the six consciousnesses, which usually face outwards to the objects of the senses, dissolving back into the base consciousness (*alayavijnana* - see section on Chittamatra doctrine below) like waves into an ocean. It then starts to move within itself creating images of subjects and objects that the mind takes to be real and experiences like waking experience. Thus, the Chittamatrins are not saying there is no difference at all between waking and dream experience. They are saying that the difference is not one of an essential difference in substance.

The Subjective Nature of Time

Maybe you are still not convinced. One knows one is awake because time is passing in a regular and predictable manner, so that one can synchronize events with an apparently stable and independent outside world. This is only another function of the stable way in which one's experience is unfolding. In fact subjectively time seems to be going fast or slow according to one's mood and situation. As for synchronizing, when events occur together they are automatically synchronized and if they do not, one thinks up a reason to explain it. If one can not, one calls it a mystery and there have been plenty of unsolved mysteries in the history of mankind.

There is a story about a man who went to a magician's home and was offered a cup of tea. He took a sip of it. What he did not know was that the magician had put a spell in the tea, so no sooner had he put his cup down than he was under the sway of a magical illusion, in which he took to his horse and rode to the end of the world where there was a great ocean so he could go no further. He met a beautiful woman whom he married and by whom he had three children. He lived with her happily for three years until, falling upon bad times, he was driven to despair and threw himself into the ocean. At that point the effect of the spell wore off and he found himself back at the magician's house with his tea still in front of him. So little time had passed, that the tea had not stopped swirling in the cup after he had put it down.

The point is that the impression of time passing and the apparent synchronicity of events does not prove that anything other than the mind itself is creating it.

It is well known, for example, that meditators can go into samadhi for hours or weeks at a time, but it does not seem to them that any time has passed at all.

Absence of Consensus

You may want to argue that there must be a world 'out there' that is not mind or there would be no consensus about what the world was like. We tend to take as real whatever the general consensus of opinion dictates, especially when it coincides with our own experience and opinions.

However, consensus is only a matter of degree. We have no means of knowing whether any of us ever sees or experiences anything in exactly the same way as anybody else. At the same time there is plenty of evidence that we do not see and experience the same thing in the same way. The difference is even more marked when one considers how differently different creatures experience the same thing. Take water for example, we experience it as something refreshing to drink. We do not normally see it as something to live in. However, fish do. A fish's view on the nature of water is totally at odds with ours. Again, take the example of someone like Mao Tse Tung. To some he appeared as a dangerous enemy and to others a dear friend. Yet to a mosquito he appeared just as a source of nourishment and to the parasites in his body a complete universe. Since for any object its every aspect is established through the perception of the moments of consciousness perceiving it, how can its existence independent of these consciousnesses be established? Consensus does not prove anything other than that certain relationships exist between different streams of experience. It does not prove that there is anything other than mind in substance.

In fact there are fundamental problems involved in positing the existence of some substance other than mind. How can such a substance be found or known? If something cannot be known without a knower, how can it ever be shown to exist independently? How does the interface between mind and matter actually work? How can matter enter into a relationship with mind, or mind with matter? Since the alternative explanation put forward by the Chittamatrins dispenses with such problems, it demands serious consideration.

Chittamatra Doctrine

In the Chittamatra School of Buddhism elaborate explanations are given of how the world appears as solid and real and 'out there', when in fact all that is occurring is transformations of a kind of mind-stuff which is like an ocean giving rise to waves. The appearance of an inner perceiving and an outer perceived aspect in each moment of consciousness gives rise to the illusion that they are different substances, mind and matter. However, matter is just an imaginary concept. Mind is empty of such a distinction between itself and what is other to it. If the meditator were to rest his mind in its own nature and see this emptiness, then all confusion would disappear and the mind would be bright, clear and self-aware. This mind is called the self-illuminating, self-aware mind (*shes pa rang rig rang gsal*). It is called this because it is the mind experiencing itself (*rang gis rang myong ba*).

As we shall see, the Madhyamikas do not accept such a mind and in their treatises they often refute the Chittamatrins on this point. However, the Chittamatrins reply that without such a mind there would be no way that one would be able to remember past events. The perceiver and perceived aspects of each moment of consciousness that has passed have gone. If nothing had experienced It and registered an impression, how could It ever be recalled? To explain the phenomena of memory and the registering of karmic traces the Chittamatrins posit the self-illuminating, self-aware mind. According to the Chittamatrins, a moment of consciousness does not consist of just a perceiving aspect and a perceived aspect: there is also the self-knowing, self-illuminating aspect. It is not a separate moment of consciousness, but it is a necessary aspect of every moment of consciousness. For example, when a flower is perceived, there is the perceived aspect, the flower, and the perceiving aspect that is focussed on the flower. The former could be called the outward-facing aspect as opposed to the inner-facing aspect that experiences and registers both the perceiving and perceived aspects of the consciousness as a whole. It is inward facing in the sense that it experiences the perceiving of the flower, registering both the flower and the consciousness but not distinguishing these as separate entities. The outward-facing aspect is like a television camera in that it films but does not register events. The inner-facing aspect does register and can be recalled or reawakened as memory. Thus the self-knowing, self-illuminating awareness is an aspect of every moment of consciousness and is what enables the *alayavijnana* (see below) to carry the traces of past events, rather like a tape-recorder registering sounds. When the right conditions arise they can be re-activated as it were. When a tape is re-played sounds are heard that correspond to the original sound enregistered on the tape. Similarly one's karma ripens to one in a way that corresponds to the original action. Although this example is not analogous in many respects, it does illustrate the principle of the ripening or re-awakening of dormant traces.

According to the Chittamatra system, the mind that realizes there are no separate perceiver and perceived entities in a moment of consciousness is the self-aware, self-illuminating aspect of each moment of consciousness. When this arises, there is no longer an appearance of such separate entities and so the base consciousness (*alayavijnana* see below) is said to be purified. At this point only the self-illuminating, self-aware aspect of consciousness arises as a pure stream of radiant, clear moments of consciousness.

The Cittamatrins were great meditators and their ideas arose from their experience through meditation (*yoga*). That is why they are often called Yogacharins. It may be that their meditation experience was as profound as in the Shentong Yogachara Madhyamaka (stage five of the progressive stages), but when they came to explain their system it was easily faulted as incoherent. Shentongpas avoid the faults of the Chittamatra system. See 'Buddha Within' for more detail (see page 146 below).

The Chittamatrins teach that there is an *alayavijnana* which is the stream of consciousness that gives rise to all six kinds of sense consciousnesses and their objects: form, sound, smell, taste, touch and mental objects.

Alayavijnana means the 'basis of all' and it is called that because all that manifests does so, on the basis of this stream of consciousness. Both the perceived and the perceiving aspect of each of the six consciousnesses are none other in substance than the *alayavijnana*. They are like the waves on an ocean. They are never other than the ocean, though they manifest differently. The *alayavijnana* is what accounts for the continuity of consciousness through life, death and rebirth, deep sleep, dreaming and the meditative absorption of a yogin. The *alayavijnana* is called the eighth consciousness.

One may wonder whether every being has his own *alayavijnana* or whether there is only one. In the relative truth each individual has his own stream of *alayavijnana* and his own actions ripen to him. In the Absolute truth there is only mind and it is empty of any separate perceivers and perceived objects.

The seventh consciousness is called the *klesha*-mind. It is a mind consciousness (the sixth type of consciousness). It is the ignorant moment of consciousness that instantaneously follows a sense consciousness, causing the outer perceived and inner perceiving aspect to appear as separate entities. The first moment of sense consciousness is free from this ignorance, but it is so swift one is not aware of it and all one's conceptual notions follow on the basis of the following moment, the *klesha*-mind. By meditating on the emptiness of a difference in substance between the inner perceiving and outer perceived aspects of consciousness the *klesha*-mind is removed and the sense consciousnesses are purified. The *alayavijana* no longer produces the illusory dualistic appearance of separate perceiving and perceived entities and so the self-aware, self-illuminating aspect of each moment shines forth unobscured.

The moments of consciousness (including both the perceiving and perceived aspect) are called the dependent nature because they arise in dependence on causes and conditions, like reflections that appear in a mirror that only arise in dependence on the objects they reflect; they are conditioned by the past actions of the person whose stream they constitute. As in the Shravaka system, the person is relative truth. The Absolute truth is the emptiness of those consciousnesses of separate, independent entities of perceiver and perceived. The separate entities which we call mind and matter are simply inventions, in other words they are the imaginary nature.

A very important element in Chittamatrin doctrine is the way it subtly divides experience into these three natures:

1. the imaginary nature (*parikalpita, kun rtag*)

2. the dependent nature (*paratantra, gzhan dbang*)

3. the truly existent nature (*parinishpanna, yongs grub*).

The Shravakas had only distinguished two kinds of reality, the relative reality of the world as we know it and the absolute reality of the *skandhas* not being self. The relative reality is like the dream experience and the absolute reality is that the person suffering in the dream is not really real. The Chittamatrins make a further distinction. The dream experience has a certain reality of its own because it is the mind, the dependent nature; that is to say the dream manifestations in themselves before one conceptualizes entities such as 'this is an enemy', 'this is a friend'. The person in the dream imagined to be something separate from the things perceived in the dream is completely imaginary, as are all the separate, independent entities that seem to appear in it; these are the imaginary nature. The absolute truth is the emptiness of the mind of these entities; this is called the truly existent nature, because that emptiness is what truly is.

Another example would be a film of a tiger or a snake. The concept of a real tiger or snake is the imaginary nature. The mere 'appearance' of the tiger or snake i.e. the light playing on the screen in the form of a tiger or snake, is real and is the dependent nature. One could also think of the screen itself as the dependent nature, like the *alayavijnana* from which all the other manifestations appear. The emptiness of the mere appearances, in the sense of their merely being light empty of any real tigers or snakes, is the truly existing nature; the screen's emptiness of real tigers and snakes is also the truly existing nature. This example is not as good as the dream example though, because it gives the impression that the screen and the light playing on it are different substances. A better example for illustrating the relationship between the *alayavijnana* and the other six consciousnesses is the ocean and the waves.

The imaginary nature is never anything but empty. The *klesha*-mind produces the concept of a basic duality and from that all other names and concepts follow. These are simply names and concepts but none of the conceptualized entities they refer to exist. They are simply imaginary. The dependent nature is real existence (*bden par grub pa*). The truly existing nature is absolute existence (*don dam grub pa*).

The dependent nature includes all the six consciousnesses and their objects, the *alayavijnana* itself and the self-illuminating, self-aware stream of consciousness that remains when the *alayavijana* is purified. The self-aware and self-illuminating stream of consciousness is empty of perceived objects as different entities to the perceiving minds and so could be called the ultimate dependent nature. The Chittamatrins thought of this as a kind of absolute, however, and this was what the Madhyamikas refuted (see Stages 3, 4 and 5 on Madhyamaka).

If you are wondering how the Chittamatrins classify phenomena into the relative and Absolute truths, the answer is that in terms of that division or classification, the self-illuminating, self-aware mind is classified as the nominal absolute (*rnam grangs pa'i don dam*). It is not classified as relative (*samvrti, kun rdzob*). However, since it arises from causes and conditions it is not the ultimate Absolute. The ultimate Absolute (*mthar thug pa'i don dam*) is the truly existent nature. The truly existent nature is simply ultimate, pure and perfect reality (yang dag pa) beyond all distinctions and conceptual grasping.

The imaginary nature is called imaginary because when one applies one's reason and examines the nature of these concepts clearly and dispassionately, one finds nothing real that corresponds to them. The dependent nature is said to be real because when one examines carefully one does find the self-illuminating, self-aware mind. The ultimate Absolute is what is found in the ultimate analysis. In the ultimate analysis one finds no perceiving and perceived entities in the mind and this is the truly existent, perfect purity and ultimate reality.

Sometimes western commentators have called Chittamatrin and Yogacharin ideas 'Idealism'. This might lead one to think that in some forms of Buddhism there is the idea of a vast limitless mind that creates the world, like a kind of creator god and that beings are all linked to this one mind as God might be to his creatures. Ideas like these have long been current in India. The *alayavijnana* is not like a God, because it is a stream of momentary consciousnesses which are not a self nor a 'Self'. The problem with ideas about God is that without the Buddhist teachings on emptiness, one could find oneself falling into the formless *samadhis* of limitless space, consciousness or nothingness. Although there is no danger of getting stuck in such a *samadhi* unless one cultivated it over a very long time, nonetheless, one should be very aware of the fact that all Buddhist *samadhis* that lead to Liberation are based on the realization of emptiness and of not self. *Samadhis* that are not so based do not lead to Liberation.

Fruit of Chittamatra

The fruit of the wisdom that sees the emptiness of the mind/matter duality is the removal of suffering (*duhkha*). Just as dark cannot exist in the presence of light, suffering cannot exist in the presence of wisdom.

The first ignorance is to take as a self what is not-self and from this arises the concept of a difference in substance between self and other. From this duality arise the afflictions (*klesha*) of attachment to what is dear and aversion to what is not dear, and through attachment and aversion the *klesha* and suffering increase.

The wisdom that sees that mind is empty of a perceiver/perceived duality (i.e. empty of outer perceived entities different in substance to the inner perceiving consciousnesses), at a single stroke, cuts through attachment and aversion and all the associated suffering. On the most subtle level every moment of consciousness is purified of all stain of ignorance and there is not even the shadow of the idea of a difference in substance between mind and its objects.

That means the mind rests free from all conceptual contrivance based on such dualistic ideas. Such ideas are based on false assertions and denials. Differences are asserted that do not exist and the true nature of reality is veiled. All our confusion is based on grasping outer objects as separate from the inner perceiving mind, and taking them to be real in a way that they are not.

By letting go of all these concepts through meditation on the mind's emptiness of this duality, the veils are cleared away and the light of the wisdom mind, the self-aware self-illuminator, is experienced. This is a very profound experience and even for those who experience it, it is difficult to explain.

Chittamatrins tried to explain it as a pure stream of self-aware moments of consciousness, but such an explanation falls into a logical contradiction (see later chapters for details). Because of this, more refined teachings on the nature of emptiness are required before one can realize the true nature of this self-aware self-illuminating experience.

Method of Examination

Reflect on how one has no proof that the outer perceived aspect (or object) of a moment of consciousness exists independently of the inner perceiving aspect. An inner perceiving aspect of a moment of consciousness cannot arise without an outer perceived aspect and vice versa. Each moment has to have both aspects simultaneously in order to arise. A perceiving consciousness with no perceived aspect of perception is a contradiction in terms, as is an object of perception with no perceiving consciousness. One cannot arise before or after the other, having an independent separate existence, just as dream appearances cannot exist independently of the dreaming mind. Each moment of the dreaming mind arises together with its dream manifestation as its object. The dream manifestation cannot appear before or after its dream consciousness, nor vice versa.

In waking life we deduce from certain patterns of relationships that objects of consciousness exist before and after we perceive them, but this is relative truth (*samvrtisatya*). When we examine closely we do not find any such existence in the ultimate analysis. Similarly, evidence offered by others, who claim to perceive the same objects as we do, does not stand up to minute analysis. We can deduce that in the relative truth others perceive the same objects as we do but ultimately every perception of both oneself and others arises and disappears simultaneously with its object. Both the outer perceived object and inner perceiving aspect of every moment of consciousness are of the same substance with no mind/matter dichotomy, just as in dreams.

Some people, who think of themselves as scientifically minded, believe that the mind is the brain or a function of the brain and that for this reason there is no essential mind/matter dichotomy.

According to their view, everything can be explained in terms of the material world. They choose to overlook the qualities of mind that have no relation to matter, such as subjective experience, thoughts and emotions. Presumably, they would not take seriously the story of Pinocchio, where a simple piece of matter, a stick, inexplicably develops a mind experiencing hopes and fears, pleasures and pain and so on. So why do they not find it strange if sub-atomic particles, atoms or molecules started to produce thoughts and feelings? There can be no scientific evidence for such a phenomenon, because it represents a semantic confusion of categories. Linguistically there is the category 'mind' and what is not mind i.e. matter. Matter, or the material world is what exists 'out there' beyond the senses. If it does not exist independent of the senses, how can it be categorised as material? How can a material world that exists outside the senses also be the senses that sense and experience it? To say that everything can be explained in terms of the material world does not answer anything. It does not even begin to address itself to the question of what conscious experience is, let alone to the question of what might or might not exist external to it.

Meditation Procedure

As with the Shravaka stage, begin by taking refuge and arousing *Bodhichitta* motivation. Reflect carefully on the example of the dream and the three natures. Reflect on how the idea of separate, truly existing outside objects is an unnecessary and superfluous invention of the mind. When you have become convinced of this rest the mind as before in the spaciousness of that emptiness. The self-illuminating, self-aware mind rests in itself, focussed on it's own nature being empty of a dualism of perceiver and perceived (*bzung 'dzin gnyis gyis stong pa*). The mind is taken as something given, so one does not focus on mind as such. One focuses on the emptiness of each moment of consciousness by not creating any concepts of there being a difference in substance between the inner perceiving aspect and outer perceived aspect. So, as in the Shravaka stage of meditation on emptiness, the mind rests in the vast expanse of emptiness.

Between sessions reflect on how all experience is like a dream. The outer world and the inner mind are all mind, just as in a dream.

Stage Three: Svatantrika Madhyamaka

Madhyamaka literally means the middle way between extremes. This can be thought of as being taught in three increasingly subtle stages. The first two stages teach the self-emptiness of the *dharmas* (referred to as Rangtong) and the last stage teaches the emptiness of what is other than conditioned *dharmas* and is referred to as Emptiness of Other (Shentong).

There are two kinds of Rangtong Madhyamaka:

1. Svatantrika Madhyamaka

2. Prasangika Madhyamaka .

Although the term "Shentong" was coined in Tibet, Madhyamaka Shentong represents the views of those whom, in India, were known as the Yogachara Madhyamikas. They call themselves the Great Madhyamikas.

The purpose of the Rangtong Madhyamaka is to establish the emptiness of self-nature of all phenomena (*dharmas*).

When we were considering the Chittamatra system we saw there were three kinds of emptiness. The emptiness of the imaginary nature, the emptiness of the dependent nature and the Emptiness that is the Truly Existent Nature.

We saw that the emptiness of the imaginary nature meant that when an imaginary object is closely scrutinized it is found not to exist at all, except in the imagination. In particular it refers to the emptiness or absence of self-entity in the person and outside objects; in other words they never existed as real entities except in the imagination.

On the other hand we saw that the emptiness of the dependent nature (which in Cittramatra refers chiefly to the mind-stream) meant it was empty of the imaginary nature but not of its own nature. This is the point that Madhyamikas refute. They do not consider the ultimate emptiness (*parinishpanna*) found by the Chittamatrins to be ultimate emptiness at all. In their opinion the Chittamatrin analysis does not go far enough.

The Shravakas, the Chittamatrins and the Madhyamaka Rangtongpas (i.e. those who follow Madhyamaka Rangtong) all agree that the mind is a stream of moments of consciousness. The Shravakas analyse it and find no self in it. The Chittamatrins further analyse the objects of consciousness and find no self-nature in them. Madhyamaka Rangtongpas further analyse the consciousnesses as well as their objects and find that neither consciousnesses nor their objects have self-nature. This absence of self-nature is absolute.

Nevertheless, all Madhyamikas agree that the mind *manifests* as a stream of moments of consciousness together with their objects, and that this simple appearance is relative truth. It is not absolute. Both Shravakas and Chittamatrins think the moments of consciousness of the mind-stream are absolute in some sense, because in the final analysis one always experiences mind as something real.

The Madhyamaka Rangtong uses reason to establish that consciousnesses and their objects cannot be absolute or ultimately real, because in the final analysis each arises only in dependence on the other and neither has a self-nature of its own.

This approach is a very powerful and profound way of establishing the emptiness of all relative phenomena that arise from causes and conditions in mutual dependence (*pratityasamutpada*). It leaves many questions unanswered, however, and in some ways the Chittamatra system gives more answers to how relative reality works than does the Madhyamaka Rangtong. Madhyamaka Rangtong is a system of reasoning that takes our everyday common sense view of the world and shows us that such a view of the world is full of logical contradictions. We experience the world through our senses and yet when we use our reason to enquire minutely into the exact mode of its existence we find nothing exists by self-nature at all.

Ultimately, experience and reason are found to be in fundamental conflict and the resolving of the conflict can only come through the direct knowledge that arises from insight meditation. Thus the aim of all Madhyamaka systems is to clarify awareness by exhausting the reasoning mind and helping it give up its preconceived ideas concerning the nature of world.

The difference between the Madhyamaka Svatantrikas and the Madhyamaka Prasangikas is that the former use arguments to refute the self-nature of phenomena (*dharmas*) and then further arguments to establish their true nature is emptiness. The Prasangikas only use arguments to refute self-nature, without trying to establish the true nature by reasoning at all. Thus the

Svatantrikas first establish that *dharmas* do not truly exist; in other words, that they have no self-nature. Then they establish that in fact their true nature is emptiness. Their arguments are very effective in refuting certain Hindu ideas according to which things do not have self-nature because their true nature is God.

To say something has no self-nature means it has no unitary, independent, lasting nature of its own. For example a rainbow appears very vividly and arises from the coming together of causes and conditions such as the sky, the rain, the sun, the angle of the light, and so on. However, when one looks closely for its ultimate nature, one finds empty space. It is as if it had disappeared under one's eyes, and yet it is still there shining brightly in the sky.

In the same way scientists study physical things like, for example, flowers. The first rough analysis breaks a flower up into its parts, petals, stamens etc. More refined analysis breaks it down into cells, molecules, then atoms, then sub-atomic particles. Finally those sub-atomic particles themselves lose their identity and become simply movement in empty space. The ultimate nature of that movement remains mysterious and hardly what you would call 'physical'.

Yet the flower remains as vivid and obvious as ever.

One has to accept, therefore, that there are two truths, the relative and the absolute. The relative is how things appear to the non-critical ordinary consciousness and the absolute is the ultimate nature of a thing that is established through accurate and minute analysis by means of the rational mind. This is the Svatantrika view.

The relative is merely concepts (*rnam rtog gis btags pa tsam*) and the absolute is emptiness free from concepts.

The Dream Example

In a dream the ultimate nature of the various things that manifest is emptiness, because none of them is real. They do not have self-nature in the sense that, for example, the dream fire does not have the nature of fire i.e. it cannot really burn anything. It is not created from the coming together of causes and conditions such as wood and matches etc.. Likewise the dream tiger cannot really bite and does not arise from the coming together of its mother and father etc. Thus the fire and the tiger do not have the self-nature of fire or of tiger. They are empty of that nature, and yet they appear and function in the sense that they can cause fear and suffering in the dreamer. Their appearing and functioning is the relative truth, but their absolute reality is emptiness.

In the same way, in waking life, relative phenomena appear and perform functions and yet, although they seem to have independent, lasting existence of their own, they have no such self-nature. Their ultimate nature is emptiness.

Svatantrikas follow the Buddha's teaching that, 'All *dharmas* are emptiness'. They take this to be the certain, true and final teaching of the Buddha concerning the ultimate nature of things i.e. they take it to be a definitive (*nitartha*) teaching. In their opinion, the Buddha's statement, 'The three realms are merely mind', needs to be carefully explained. In other words it is a provisional (*neyartha*) teaching. They interpret the statement that everything is mind to mean that the relative is merely concepts. They do not accept, as the Chittamatrins do, that in the ultimate analysis there is a truly existing substance, mind. The point they are criticizing about the Chittamatra is that, since a moment of consciousness arises in dependence on an object of consciousness and vice versa, consciousness cannot exist independently with its own self-nature, so the mind that the Chittamatrins are positing must be relative, not ultimately real or absolute. By arguing in this way the Svantantrikas are more thorough and precise in their analysis of the absolute nature of things. They establish very forcefully that the ultimate nature of all relative *dharmas* is emptiness because they are all merely concepts. Even concepts such as "emptiness" itself can be established as being empty.

Although some Svatantrikas teach the two truths as quite separate and different in nature, others stress that they are inseparable, both being different aspects of a single reality. The former are stressing that emptiness means absolute non-existence and that all that we experience as existing is relative truth. The latter are stressing that even though this is true, emptiness and appearance cannot ultimately be two separate entities. Ultimately the true nature of things cannot be conceptualized as either existent, non-existent, both or neither. Such a view is very close to the Prasangika view. The main difference is that Prasangikas do not use logical argument to establish the absolute empty nature of the *dharmas*, whereas Svatantrikas do.

Method of Investigation

Svatantrikas use many detailed arguments for establishing their position. The object is to establish the emptiness of all elements of existence, and the method is systematically to examine each element of existence in turn until one reaches the conviction that all without exception are empty.

In the *Prajnaparamita sutras* the Buddha lists 108 emptinesses starting with the eighteen elements and including all phenomena up to the ten powers and the Omniscient Wisdom of the Buddha.

In Buddhist philosophy the elements of existence are classified in several different ways; each system purports to cover all possible elements of existence or experience. The idea is to have a kind of check list of all possible phenomena and then to examine them all to find their ultimate true nature that is common to them all.

We have already seen how the five *skandhas* are used in this way. Now we are going to use the eighteen elements as another example of this method.

The eighteen elements are: eye, form, eye consciousness, ear, sound, ear consciousness, nose, smell, nose consciousness, tongue, taste, tongue consciousness, body, tactile sensation, body consciousness, mind, mental objects, mind consciousness.

In this list the six sense organs, 'eye' etc., refer to the actual sensitive part of each organ that links the physical or mental object to the consciousness. Eye consciousness cannot arise simply in the presence of form, the light sensitive organ has also to be present and functioning. The mind 'organ' is the moment of consciousness that bears the image of a sense consciousness or a mental object and enables a conceptual consciousness to grasp it.

Nagarjuna was the great founder of the Madhyamaka system. In his *Mulamadhyamaka-karika* he sums up his system of reasoning. His disciple Buddhapalita wrote a famous commentary on this, but his contemporary, Bhavaviveka criticized his method and established a system of his own, again based on the *Mulamadhyama-karika*. In this way he became the founder of the Svatantrika Madhyamaka. Chandrakirti, a follower of Buddhapalita wrote a treatise defending Buddhapalita and arguing against Bhavaviveka's critique of his work. In this way he became the founder of the Prasangika Madhyamaka.

So what kind of reasoning did Nagarjuna use to establish the emptiness of all *dharmas*? I am not going to go into them all here. In fact, for the meditator it is not really necessary to know them all. One just has to know enough to be able to establish the emptiness of all *dharmas* for oneself as a preparation for the meditation.

One of the most powerful arguments he used was the argument against a phenomenon being either single or multiple. Taking each element in turn, he asked if it could be said to exist as a single entity or an entity made up of parts? It is taken as axiomatic that anything that exists must be either single or multiple, since no other possibility exists. Take, for example, a form such as the hand. If it were single it could not be divided; since it can be divided it must be multiple. However, once you have divided the hand into its parts, where is the hand? One does not find a hand as such, so the hand cannot exist; it is neither single nor multiple. 'Hand' is nothing in itself. It has no self-nature. It is simply a concept. You may think to yourself that although it is true that there is no hand as such, there are the atoms that make up the hand. However, an atom has to be either single or multiple. If it were single it could not have dimensions. To have dimensions means it has a left and a right side etc. One can find all the parts, but then where is the atom itself? However minutely one analyses, one can never arrive at a smallest possible existent particle of which all other existent things could be said to be made up. Nagarjuna used reasoning to establish this; modern day scientists are coming to the same conclusion using experiments. Maybe we find the experimental evidence more convincing than Nagarjuna's reasoning. It does not really matter which method one uses if the conclusion is the same.

Nagarjuna applied the same argument to mental phenomena. Mental phenomena are experienced by the mind. Is a moment of experience single or multiple? If it is neither it cannot truly exist. If it were single it would not be able to have any duration. Duration means there is a beginning, middle and end. If you say there is a beginning, middle and end to a moment, then the moment is three moments and the original moment has disappeared. Therefore it cannot be either single or multiple. However minutely you analyse you never find a smallest possible truly existent moment of experience of which all other existent experience could be made up. Consciousness or experience is empty of self-nature, because ultimately there is no truly existing moment of consciousness or experience.

Svatantrikas like to use two main types of argument. One is the argument used above i.e. neither single nor multiple and the other is mere dependent arising (*pratityasamutpada*). What is dependently arising by definition has no self-nature. Therefore to show all phenomena are dependently arising is to show they have no self-nature.

NB. Some Svatantrikas take outer appearing objects to be different in substance to the mind and some do not, but all agree that both outer perceived objects and inner perceiving consciousnesses are empty of self-nature. None of them accept (as Cittamatrins do) that dependently arising phenomena have a kind of true existence.

Meditation Procedure

In the Chittamatra meditation, we saw that the thing that was empty (*stong gzhi*) was the mind, empty of perceiver/perceiver duality. In the Svatantrika meditation the thing that is empty is all phenomena, inner and outer, i.e. both mental phenomena as well as outer appearing objects. Everything is empty of self-nature.

Begin the meditation session with taking Refuge and arousing *Bodhichitta*. Then, having established certitude by listening, studying and reflecting, abandon all doubts and rest the mind in its own emptiness and the emptiness of all phenomena free from all concepts such as existence, non-existence and so on. Rest the mind in that vast open space, and, just as when one recognizes dreams for what they are they disappear, so everything disappears into the vast expanse of emptiness when one meditates free from conceptual contrivance (*nishprapancha*).

Between sessions meditate on how things vividly appear but are empty and how, though empty, they appear, as dreams appear even though they are empty.

This emptiness is the nature of the Buddha's Dharmakaya and also the ultimate nature of all beings. Because of this sameness of nature, beings are able to realize the Enlightenment of Buddhas and become Buddhas with the power to work for ever at the task of liberating all sentient beings.

Thinking of this one dedicates all the merit accumulated through meditating like this to the complete and perfect Enlightenment of beings.

Stage Four: Prasangika Madhyamaka

The Svatantrika system is very effective for a first understanding of emptiness because it cuts through one's attachment to things as real. However, even though the Svatantrikas themselves think they teach an understanding that goes beyond concepts, from the Prasangika point of view their understanding is still subtly conceptual. The Prasangikas argue that to establish emptiness through reasoning is a subtle attempt to grasp the ultimate nature with the conceptual mind. Reason shows the conceptual mind is always in error; it can only ever give a distorted and ultimately self-contradictory version of experience, never the nature of reality itself. Therefore they refuse to use any reasoning to establish the true nature of phenomena. They say that since the ultimate nature is beyond even the most subtle concepts (*nishprapancha*), it is misleading to try to establish or prove *nishprapancha* as a description or a concept that expresses the ultimate nature of reality.

They are adamant in not positing anything either positive or negative. Some argue that this is a dishonest view in the sense that one is simply side-stepping issues and refusing to allow opponents to refute one's views. However, there is something very profound in this method. It is quite uncompromising in its systematic refutation of all conceptual attempts to grasp the nature of the absolute. The original Prasangikas in India and Tibet did not assert anything about the relative appearance of phenomena either. They considered the nature of this also to be beyond even the most subtle concepts of existence, non-existence etc.

Some later Prasangikas, namely the Gelugpa school of Tibet, do hold views concerning the nature of relative phenomena. They establish through reasoning that relative phenomena exist conventionally (*vyavahara, tha snyad du*). Other Prasangikas are very doubtful that such a system can be considered Prasangika at all. A number of very powerful refutations of the Gelugpa view have been made by both Gelugpa and other scholars and debate still continues to this day, even now as the Dharma spreads to the West. The debate will certainly continue here. Maybe western scholars will resolve it, where Tibetans have failed to do so.

We will only be considering the original Prasangika view in this meditation progression on Emptiness. That is, we will confine ourselves to refuting all views, but not asserting any counter-argument establishing any view of our own. This amounts to a complete destruction of all conceptual views, leaving one with no alternative other than a non-conceptual view of the nature of reality. The aim of the Prasangika is to silence completely the conceptual mind, allowing the mind to rest in absolute freedom from concepts. Absolute freedom from concepts is what Prasangikas call emptiness. The absolute nature of reality is emptiness in that sense only. It cannot be established as empty, or even as freedom from concepts (*nisprapanca*) by the conceptual mind because that would not be true emptiness or true freedom from concepts. It would still be just concepts.

Finally, therefore, the Prasangikas are not saying anything about the ultimate nature of reality or of emptiness. That is not the aim of their system. Their aim is to free the awareness of its conceptualizing habit and to let the ultimate nature of reality reveal itself in a totally non-conceptual way. It is a very powerful system in that it gives the conceptual mind nothing to grasp onto at all. In contrast to the Svatantrika, which is good for refuting non-Buddhist systems, the Prasangika is very good for refuting subtle views held in other Buddhist systems. It shows how, although they all claim to go beyond concepts, they still have subtle concepts as long as they try to establish the nature of reality through reason and the use of concepts.

The Dream Example

The Svatantrika view is like realizing that the dream fire or dream tiger are not real. In this way there is the subtle concept of a real emptiness and an unreal fire or tiger. In other words there is a subtle conceptual division between the absolute and the relative truths. The Prasangika view is like realizing the true nature of the dream fire or dream tiger directly, without first negating the dream and establishing emptiness. If there is no concept of 'real', there is no concept, 'unreal'. If there is no concept, 'self-nature', there is no concept, 'absence of self-nature'. Thus the mind rests in total peace without any conceptual contrivance whatever. The dream tiger does not need the concept of emptiness to negate a reality it never had.

This is obviously a much more advanced way of practising than that of the Svatantrika. For an ordinary person it is not possible to gain a non-conceptual understanding of emptiness immediately. It is very good to use the Svatantrika approach to establish emptiness at first. This cuts through one's ordinary conceptual way of thinking, which takes existence and non-existence for granted. Then one has to use the Prasangika to cut through the conceptual mind completely. It enables one to cut through the tendency to separate the relative truth of how things appear from the absolute truth of how they actually are. As long as one separates the two truths, one's understanding of emptiness is subtly conceptual. Once one lets go of the tendency to subtly divide the two truths, one sees the relative as naturally empty. It is like seeing dreams naturally as they are without contrivance or confusion. Then one sees that relative truth and absolute truth are just names for two aspects of one reality. Even the terms relative and absolute are conceptual creations. Ultimately there is no such distinction.

In a dream many things appear that are empty. If they are empty and not real, how can their empty essence be real? To hold a concept that the ultimate nature of the dream appearances is emptiness is not to see their nature properly. The awareness must rest meditatively without creating any concepts of real or unreal, empty or not-empty, existent or not existent etc.

Until that non-conceptual nature has been discovered, however, it is not possible to avoid subtle positive and negative concepts. That is why it is useful to go through all the stages of this meditation progression on Emptiness. At each stage you will learn to recognize and familiarize yourself with all the subtle concepts that are going to creep into your meditation again and again.

Recognizing them, you will see their nature more and more clearly and eventually the mind will tire of them.

Just as darkness cannot exist in the presence of light, ignorance cannot exist in the presence of awareness that rests without concepts. At first the mind rests like that for just brief moments at a time, but gradually, by recognizing the significance and importance of these moments, they are fostered and as the conceptual tendencies grow weaker, the non-conceptual awareness grows stronger and stronger, like the sun emerging from behind clouds.

Method of Investigation

Chandrakirti was the great proponent of the Prasangika system, and he relied a lot on arguments that showed that *dharmas* did not arise. If *dharmas* can be shown never to arise, it goes without saying that they do not abide or perish and that they have no self-nature. Shantarakshita, a Svatantrika, on the other hand, argued in his *Madhyamakalamkara* that if you can show that things have no self-nature, it is easy to show they do not arise, stay or perish.

Chandrakirti used the argument that inner and outer things do not arise from themselves, from something other than themselves, from both or from neither i.e. causelessly. Since that covers all four possibilities, this argument shows that nothing truly arises. For something to arise, it first has to be absent. A non-Buddhist school of thought, the Samkhyas, believed that things arose from themselves. Chandrakirti refuted this saying that if something already existed it would not need to arise. Arising has no meaning for something which already exists. The Hinayana Buddhist schools, the Vaibhasikas and Sautrantikas, believed that things arose from what was other than themselves. In other words one moment gave rise to the next. Chandrakirti argued that no connection exists between one moment and the next. A moment arises at the very instant that the moment before disappears. Something that has no connection with another thing can hardly be called its cause, otherwise one could say darkness was the cause of light or light the cause of darkness, just because the one followed on from the other.

Since, in this way things arising from themselves and things arising from something else are refuted, one might try to argue that things arise from both. The Jains thought this. Chandrakirti argued that such a position has the faults of both the previous positions.

Maybe one would like to argue that things arise from nothing? This would be like the belief of those who deny all cause and effect, including karma cause and effect. Such a school existed in India. They were called the Ajivakas and Chandrakirti refuted their view by saying that if things arose without cause what would be the point of doing anything? For example, why should a farmer bother to plant his crops, if causes do not bring about effects? Such a belief, which suggests that everything is haphazard and chaotic, is totally non-scientific.

Maybe a film is a good example of how things are non-arising. We all know that when we see a moving film it is really a series of still frames being projected onto the screen in very quick succession. It may look as if one thing is affecting another thing on the screen, but, in fact, except for the sequential arrangement, there is no connection between them. There are even gaps between the pictures. For something to cause something else there has to be a point where they meet, otherwise how could the one affect the other? But a cause never exists at the same time as its effect. Once the effect has arisen the cause is in the past. The cause has to precede its effect, otherwise cause has no meaning. If they arise together at the same moment they cannot be cause and effect. In the Prasangika system this argument is developed in detail and at great length. Although we have not looked at it in detail here, we have seen, at least, the kind of reasoning used.

It is important to understand that what is being argued about here is the ultimate nature of things. Of course, on a gross level, everyone has to agree that, for example, a candle flame arises from the wick and wax of the candle and from the wood and flame of a match and so on. It is when one examines the concept of causality very minutely that it begins to fall apart, and this is what the Prasangikas are interested in. As to the way apparent causality works in the world, the Prasangika does not claim to have anything to add to what the world says about it. However, for the

Prasangika the arising of things is mere relative appearance. There is no arising in the absolute. As in dreams, relatively things appear to arise, but they do not arise in the ultimate analysis. The Prasangika does not hold the position that either the absolute or the relative arise or do not arise, exist or do not exist etc.

The Prasangikas are very careful to emphasize that as well as things not being truly existent (*bden par grub*), and not arising (*skye ba*), they are also not not truly existing (*bden par ma grub*) and not non-arising (*skye ba med pa*). Such positions are equally unsatisfactory, because if true existence does not exist, then neither can its opposite, not true existence, since that only has meaning in relation to existence. If similarly there is no arising, there is no non-arising. In this way they make sure that all concepts, positive and negative, are negated and that nothing is asserted in their place. In other words the Prasangika system is beyond any mental grasping whatsoever (*blo'i 'dzin gtang thams cad las 'das pa*).

Incidentally, when it is said that the Prasangika holds no position or view it means he does not truly believe any view or position or hold anything as his absolute and final opinion. It does not mean that Chandrakirti, for example, could not say 'I'm Chandrakirti and I live in Nalanda'. Just saying something does not mean that one holds it as ultimately true.

The reason we have not dwelt at length here on all the detailed arguments used by Chandrakirti and other commentators is that we are talking about the meditator's approach. Jamgon Kontrul Rinpoche, in his

Encyclopaedia of Knowledge, in the chapter on *shamatha* and *vipashyana* explains that the meditator only needs to analyse intellectually very briefly, just enough to convince himself of the way to meditate. Then he should drop all doubt and intellectual enquiry and rest his mind naturally without any conceptual contrivance. Of course, if one still has doubts one will have to return again and again to the study and reflective stages of the practice. When actually meditating, however, one must let all doubts subside and rest the mind without artifice.

Base, Path and Fruit

The base for both Svatantrika and Prasangika Madhyamaka is the two truths, the path is the two accumulations (*sambhara, tshogs*) and the fruit is the two *kayas* (Buddha bodies).

For the Prasangika, during the meditation session one rests one's mind without conceptual effort on the inseparable two truths. One does not cling to any concept of good, bad, happy, sad etc. Even time has no meaning. Some people get very attached to time and think it is very important how long they meditate and so on. This can become a great obstacle to realizing the non-contrived state. Time itself never arises. To meditate like this is to accumulate wisdom (*jnanasambhara, yeshes tshogs*).

Between sessions, however, one has to deal with one's everyday life. Here we see cause and effect working all the time. They may not ultimately arise but they appear to do so to the conceptual mind, so it is important to respect that and not to confuse the levels of the teaching. Between sessions there is good and bad, skilful and unskilful actions that lead to happiness and suffering respectively. So it is very important to use this time for performing good actions like serving the Triple Gem, giving help where needed and so on. This is called the accumulation of good (*punyasambhara, bsod nams tshogs*) for the benefit of all beings.

Although this path is called the path of the two accumulations, in the last analysis there is no accumulation, no path and no fruit. The mind is naturally free from mental constructions. There is nothing to add or remove. This is emptiness without any sense of negating anything and without any concept of emptiness. The mind just rests naturally in its natural state without contrivance.

The fruit is the two bodies (*kayas*) of Buddha. These are the *Dharmakaya* and the form *kayas*. Samsara is conceptual elaboration (*rnam rtog spros pa, prapancha*), Nirvana is absence of conceptual elaboration (*nishprapancha*). Although the *Dharmakaya* is the cessation of all conceptual elaboration, on the path to Buddhahood, the Bodhisattvas make vows and wishes out of compassion for beings, and through the power of their compassion, the results of their past vows and the pure karma of beings they are able to manifest form bodies when they reach Buddhahood. These form bodies are in essence free from conceptual elaboration, but because of the concepts of beings they are able to appear to them. They appear to their pure vision, but they are not the absolute Buddha.

Method of Meditation

For this meditation the mind should be very relaxed. Having taken Refuge and aroused *Bodhichitta*, let the mind rest, vast and spacious, like clear and empty space. Whenever the mind gets tense from too much studying and so on, one should let the mind rest naturally without contrivance in the natural non-contrived emptiness of mind. This is the way to relax the mind. If you have understood the non-contrived state correctly, you will find all tension and emotional disturbance subsides, like ocean waves becoming still by themselves. Whenever strong passions like anger, desire or jealousy arise, letting the mind rest without contrivance is sufficient remedy, without doing anything at all. They simply subside and come to rest by themselves. Similarly with suffering, if one rests in its essence without contrivance, that sensation of suffering becomes spaciousness and peace.

It is important also to rest the mind like this when the mind is happy, otherwise, one will lose one's equanimity at the point of change when the happiness comes to an end.

Stage Five: Shentong Emptiness-of-Other

This stage could also be called Yogachara Madhyamaka or Great Madhyamaka. As was mentioned in the last section, many Shentong masters criticize the Prasangika Madhyamikas for their claim that they do not hold any views. In the opinion of these masters, Prasangikas just dodge the issue because they refute everyone else's views and then avoid the refutation of their own views by claiming not to have any.

From the Shentong point of view, the fault with both Svatantrika and Prasangika Madhyamaka is that they do not distinguish between the three different kinds of existence, the three different kinds of emptiness and the three different kinds of absence of essence that correspond to the three natures (i.e. the imaginary, dependent and perfect existence). Some Shentong masters argue that Rangtong Madhyamaka teaches only the first kind of emptiness, in other words, the emptiness of the imaginary nature, which is simply its complete non-existence. They argue that if this kind of emptiness were the absolute reality, or if mere absence of conceptual contrivance were absolute reality, it would be a mere nothingness, empty space. How can mere nothingness account for the manifestations of samsara and nirvana? They appear vividly as impure and pure manifestations respectively. Mere emptiness does not account for this. There has to be some element that is in some sense luminous, illuminating and knowing.

Because Shentongpas makes the same distinction between the three natures as the Chittamatrins do, and because they stress the true existence of the luminous knowing aspect of mind, many Rangtong masters have confused it with Chittamatra.

However, there are very important differences between Chittamatra and Shentong. Firstly, Shentongpas do not accept the Chittamatra view that consciousness (*vijnana)* is truly existent. They hold the Madhyamaka view that it is non-arising and without self-nature. They consider themselves to be the Great Madhyamikas because their system involves not only recognizing freedom from all conceptual contrivance, but also the realization of the Wisdom Mind (jnana) that is free from all conceptual contrivance.

This non-conceptual Wisdom Mind is not the object of the conceptualizing process and so is not negated by Madhyamaka reasoning. Therefore, it can be said to be the only thing that has absolute and true existence.

It is important to understand that this true existence does not mean that it is the object of conceptualization. If it were even the most subtle object of the conceptual process, it could be refuted by Prasangika reasoning. The non-conceptual Wisdom Mind is not something that even supreme wisdom (*prajna*) can take as its object. Anything that can be an object of consciousness, however pure and refined, is dependently arising and has no true existence.

So what is the non-conceptual Wisdom Mind? It is something that one realizes through means other than the conceptual process. One experiences it directly just as it is and any conceptual fabrication obscures it. All the teachings of Mahamudra and Maha Ati and the whole of the Tantras are about this non-conceptual Wisdom Mind and the means of realizing it. For this realization a Guru is absolutely necessary. The Guru's realization and the disciple's devotion and openness of mind have to meet in such a way that the disciple can experience that non-conceptual Wisdom Mind directly. From then on the disciple uses that experience as the basis of his practice, nurturing and fostering it until it becomes clear and stable. Only then can the final, full and perfect realization occur.

From the Shentong point of view, what the Chittamatrins call absolute i.e. the experience of the self-knowing, self-illuminating awareness, is wrongly interpreted by them to be a consciousness (*vijnana*). Shentong says that although it is true that when the mind rests in emptiness without conceptual contrivance (which all Mahayanists claim to do) one does experience the clear luminosity and aware quality of mind, this is not a consciousness (*vijnana*). *Vijnana* means a divided consciousness; in other words divided into a seeing and seen aspect. Shentongpas take it as a fact that a mind bounded by concepts of time and space, must in some sense entertain the concepts of moments having duration and atoms with extension in space. Furthermore, it will always seem that for an instant of knowing to take place, a knowing and a known aspect of consciousness must arise, even if it is understood that they have no ultimate or real existence.

Shentongpas regard the concept of a stream of consciousness consisting of moments having knowing and known aspects as a misunderstanding of reality. It is a false or deceptive 'reality' or 'truth'. In fact the term relative truth we have been using throughout this text is a translation of the Sanskrit word, *samvrti'*, which means covered or concealed; the Tibetan translation, *kun rdzob*, means dressed up or blown up to give a false appearance. One could say *samvrti* is mere concealment (*samvrti*) or merely apparently true. In a certain sense it is not reality or truth at all, but merely a seeming reality. It is only relatively true in the sense that things seem to be that way to ordinary beings. Ultimately it is not true at all.

From the Shentong point of view, the luminous self-aware non-conceptual mind that is experienced in meditation, when the mind is completely free from concepts, is Absolute Reality, and not a *vijnana*; *vijnana* is always *samvrti* from the Shentong point of view and is not what is found by the supreme wisdom (*prajna*) that sees Absolute Reality. When the luminous, self-aware, non-conceptual Mind that is the Wisdom Mind (jnana) is realized by the supreme Wisdom (*prajna*) there is no seeing and seen aspect, no realizing and realized aspect to the realization. This is called the Transcendence of Supreme Wisdom (*Prajnaparamita*). It is none other than the non-conceptual Wisdom Mind (jnana) itself. It is also called the non-dual Wisdom Mind (jnana), the Clear Light (*prabhasvara*) Nature of Mind and Dhatu (spacious expanse or element). Elsewhere it is called the Element (*dhatu, dbyings)* and Awareness inseparable, Clarity and Emptiness inseparable, Bliss and Emptiness inseparable. It is also called the *Dharmata* and the *Tathagatagarbha*.

Shentongpas contend that the experience of complete freedom from conceptual contrivance (*nishprapancha*) must also be the experience of the Clear Light Nature of Mind. In their opinion a Prasangika who denies this must still have some subtle concept, which is obscuring or negating this Reality; in other words such a person has not truly realized complete freedom from conceptual contrivance. This happens because for a long time the meditator has been cutting through illusion and seeing emptiness as a kind of negation. This becomes such a strong habit that even when the experience of Absolute Reality, the Clear Light Nature of Mind, starts to break through like the sun from behind clouds, meditators automatically turn their mind towards it to subtly negate it. Shentongpas argue that if there really were no conceptual contrivance in the mind the Clear Light Nature would shine forth so clearly and unmistakably that it would not be possible to deny it.

The fact that the Rangtong Madhyamikas do deny it, shows the importance of the third Wheel of the Doctrine. The Buddha is said to have turned the Wheel of the Doctrine (*Dharmachakra*) three times. That is to say, he gave three major cycles of teaching. The first corresponded to the Shravaka level of meditation on emptiness, the second to the Madhyamaka Rangtong level, and the third to the Madhyamaka Shentong. Each level of teaching remedies the faults in the level below it. Thus Shentongpas regard the third Wheel of the Doctrine as remedying the faults in the second, the Madhyamaka Rangtong.

The third Wheel of the Doctrine is explained in detail in the *Tathagatagarbha Sutras* and these are commented on in the *Mahayanaottaratantrashastra* (also known as the *Ratnagotravibhaga*) which in the Tibetan tradition is attributed to Maitreya. Here it is taught that the *Tathagatagarbha* pervades all beings and that the Mind's nature is the Clear Light. These are two ways of saying the same thing. The classic examples given are those of butter in milk, gold in gold ore and sesame oil in sesame seeds. The butter, gold and sesame oil pervade in the sense that when the milk, gold ore or sesame seeds are processed, the butter, gold and sesame oil emerge.

In the same way beings go through a process of purification from which the purified Buddha Nature (*Tathagatagarbha*) emerges.

If the true nature (*dharmata*) of beings were not the *Tathagatagarbha* they could never become Buddhas, in the same way that a rock that did not contain gold could never yield gold however much it were to be refined.

Purpose of Teaching the *Tathagatagarbha*

The purpose of teaching the *Tathagatagarbha* is to give meditators confidence that they already have Buddha Nature. Without such confidence it is very difficult to fully rest the mind free from all conceptual contrivance, because there is always a subtle tendency to try to remove or achieve something.

In the *Ratnagotravibhaga* five reasons are given for teaching the *Tathagatagarbha*. Firstly, it encourages those who would otherwise be so self-depreciating that they would not even try to arouse *Bodhichitta* and attain Buddhahood. Secondly, it humbles those who, having aroused *Bodhichitta*, feel intrinsically superior to others who have not. Thirdly, it removes the fault of taking the stains, which are unreal, to be the true nature of beings. Fourthly, it removes the fault of taking the Clear Light Nature, which is real, to be unreal. Fifthly, by showing that all beings are intrinsically of the same nature as the nature of Buddha, it removes the obstacle to the arising of true compassion, which sees no difference between self and others.

Base, Path and Fruit

Since the Buddha Nature is without beginning, it is present in the base, path and fruit. The only difference between the three stages is that the base is the time when the Buddha Nature is completely obscured by stains, the path is when it is partially purified and the fruit is when it is completely purified.

The Doctrine of the *Ratnagotravibhaga*

The *Ratnagotravibhaga* gives three points of Mahayana Buddhist doctrine that demonstrate all sentient beings have *Tathagatagarbha*. It lays out the doctrine on *Tathagatagarbha* under ten headings and it gives the nine examples from the *Tathagatagarbhasutra* which illustrate how, although the *Tathagatagarbha* remains unchanged, the veils have to be removed.

It teaches three stages, the pure, the partly pure and the completely pure, which correspond to beings, Bodhisattvas and Buddhas respectively. These correspond to the base, path and fruit *Tathagatagarbha*.

At first, ordinary beings do not recognize the Clear Light Nature of mind at all. It is therefore covered with both gross and subtle veils; this is the base *Tathagatagarbha*, which is like gold when it is still in the gold ore.

Once the true nature of the mind has been recognized by the Bodhisattva, the gross veils fall away. From then on Bodhisattvas use their realization as the essence of the path, which consists of refining it as one refines gold once it has been separated from the ore.

The final realization is the fruit *Tathagatagarbha* and is like the perfectly refined gold that has all the qualities of pure gold. The fruit *Tathagatagarbha* displays all the qualities of a perfectly Enlightened Buddha.

Ratnagotravibhaga 1.154 teaches that the Element (i.e. the *Tathagatagarbha*) is empty of what is contingent (i.e. the stains) that are separable, since they are not of its essence, but not empty of our innate Buddha qualities that are not separable, since they are of its essence.

Our innate Buddha qualities are the qualities of the non-conceptual Wisdom Mind, which, when it is purified, is called the *Dharmakaya*. When the Wisdom Mind is not purified the qualities are not manifest and it is called *Tathagatagarbha*.

These qualities are inseparable from that Wisdom Mind. They are not divisible from its essence as if the mind's essence were one thing and the qualities another. If they were like that they would have been shown to be empty of own nature by Madhyamaka reasoning. The essence would have arisen dependent on the qualities and the qualities dependent on the essence. Such qualities or such an essence could not have any self-nature or true existence. However, the Buddha qualities are not like this. They cannot be grasped by the conceptual mind and are not separable from the essence of the Wisdom Mind (which also cannot be grasped by the conceptual mind). Thus the Buddha qualities are not compounded or conditioned phenomena, which arise, stay and perish. They exist primordially.

Shentongpas criticize the view of the other Madhyamikas who say that the Buddha's qualities arise as a result of the good deeds, vows and connections made by Bodhisattvas on the path to Enlightenment. If the qualities arose in this way then they would be compounded and impermanent phenomena and not beyond samsara. The whole point of Buddhism is that the Buddha is beyond samsara. Shentongpas accept the doctrine of the *Tathagatagarbha sutras* that the Buddha qualities are primordially existent. Nevertheless, good deeds, vows and connections are necessary for removing veils.

Both the Chittamatrins (and Rangtong Madhyamikas who have a philosophical view) think of the Buddha's wisdom as a stream of moments of purified awareness that has emptiness or the conception-less nature as its subtle object. Since the object is pure, the awareness itself exhibits the qualities of a pure mind and this is called jnana. Its arising is associated automatically with the qualities of the Buddha that result from the actions of the Bodhisattva on his path to Enlightenment through his accumulation of wisdom and merit (*punya*). Therefore, whether they express this view explicitly or not, the Rangtong Madhyamikas who have a view regard the Buddha qualities as relative phenomena whose essence is emptiness.

As has been mentioned already above, Shentongpas do not accept that the Wisdom Mind knows in a dualistic way. It does not divide into a knowing and a known aspect, so there is no subtle object of the Wisdom Mind. It is not a stream of moments of awareness. It is completely unbounded and free from all concepts including time and space. Therefore it is primordially existent like its qualities.

The Doctrine of the *Mahayanasutralamkara*

This is another of the five Treatises that the Tibetan tradition attributes to Maitreya.

The *Mahayanasutralamkara* teaches a distinction between the *dharmin* and the *Dharmata*. *Dharmin* is a general term that refers to that which has the particular quality or *dharma* under discussion. In this context the relative mind is the *dharmin* that has as its essence the *Dharmata* – the quality under discussion. *Dharmata* means that which is the true nature, the absolute Clear Light Mind.

The relative mind is mistaken and confused, while the absolute mind is non-mistaken and non-confused. The relative mind faces out towards its object and has a perceiving and perceived aspect. It constitutes the stain that is to be given up. Its essence or true nature is the Clear Light Mind.

Thus the relative mind is the thing that is empty of something (*stong gzhi*). It is empty of self-nature. Its real nature is the absolute Clear Light Nature.

According to Shentongpas the Clear Light Mind in the *Mahayanasutralamkara* is the same as the *Tathagatagarbha* in the *Ratnagotravibhaga*. The relative mind is what is referred to as the stains in the *Ratnagotravibhaga*. However the *Ratnagotravibhaga* does not explicitly say the true nature of the stains is the *Tathagatagarbha*. It just says they are empty of self-nature. Thus there is a slight difference in the lay-out, but the meaning is the same.

The Doctrine of the *Madhyantavibhaga*

This is another of the Five Treatises of Maitreya. This text is interpreted by Shentongpas as alluding to the following doctrine which is found clearly expounded in the *Sandhinirmochana sutra*.

i. the three modes of existence,

ii. the three modes of emptiness,

iii. the three modes of absence of essence.

The Three Modes of Existence.

The imaginary nature exists as mere conceptual creations. It is the objects that our concepts and ideas refer to. For example, since the real tiger in a dream is non-existent, it is merely a figment of the imagination. In other words, the imaginary nature, which refers to the contents of the delusion rather than the delusion itself, exists only in the imagination as the referent of names and concepts. For example we talk about past events. These events do not exist at all. They are simply names or concepts for referring to things that are being imagined, but which do not exist. Objects external to the mind and senses are of this nature. They do not exist and yet names and concepts are applied to them.

The dependent nature substantially exists (*rdzas su yod pa*) in the sense that it is not just imaginary in the above sense. Thus the thoughts, concepts, names and ideas themselves, that appear both to the mind and in it, do actually occur. For example, the dream tiger occurs and produces an effect, such as fear, in the dreaming mind. However, the dream tiger is only substantial in relation to the real tiger that is imagined to be there. It is not substantial in an absolute sense. From the Shentong point of view, it is not enough just to refute the true existence of the imaginary nature. Shentongpas use Madhyamaka reasoning to refute the true existence of the dependent nature as well as of the imaginary nature.

The perfectly existent nature truly exists because it exists in a non-conceptual way. In the Chittamatra the perfectly existent nature is said to be mere emptiness, in the sense of freedom from the conceptual process of distinguishing outer perceived objects as different in substance to the inner perceiving mind. Shentongpas say it is the non-conceptual Wisdom Mind itself. It is indeed empty of the conceptual process of distinguishing outer perceived objects as different in substance to the inner perceiving minds. It is also empty of the conceptualizing process that creates the appearance of a divided consciousness (*vijnana*) i.e. a stream of discrete moments of consciousness with perceiving and perceived aspects. It is completely free from any conceptualizing process and knows in a way that is completely foreign to the conceptual mind. It is completely unimaginable in fact. That is why it can be said to truly exist.

ii. The Three Modes of Emptiness

The imaginary nature is empty in the sense that it does not exist at all. It is the emptiness of something non-existent. The referents of names and concepts, the conceived objects themselves, never exist except in the imagination. They have no self-nature of their own, so they are said to be empty in themselves.

Some Shentong masters say that the emptiness taught by the Rangtong is nothing more than this. In other words they do not regard it as being the ultimate emptiness taught by the Shentongpas.

The dependent nature is empty in the sense of something existent, but not ultimately existent. In the relative it exists and functions, having its own characteristic. It is empty of the imaginary nature but not empty of itself. This is like the Chittamatra view. In absolute terms, according to the Shentong view, the dependent nature does not exist at all. It is empty of self-nature because it is dependently arising. However, the appearance of the dependent nature is only possible because in essence all appearance is the Mind's Clear Light Nature and this does exist ultimately.

The perfectly existent nature is the ultimate absolute emptiness. It is the non-conceptual Wisdom Mind, non-arising, non-abiding and non-perishing. It is primordially existent and endowed with qualities. It is empty in the sense that it is free from all the obscuration created by the conceptual mind. Therefore when the conceptual mind tries to grasp it, it finds nothing and so it experiences it as emptiness. Thus, it is empty to the conceptual mind, but from its own point of view it is the Clear Light Nature of Mind together with all its qualities.

iii. The Three Modes of Absence of Essence.

The imaginary nature is without essence in the sense that it does not exist through having to its own characteristic. For example the imaginary fire does not have the characteristics of fire which is hot and burning. In the same way every phenomenon that is a conceived object of a concept does not exist with its own characteristic.

The dependent nature is without essence in the sense that it never arises. Shentongpas refute the existence of the dependent nature by using Madhyamaka reasoning.

The perfectly existent nature is absolute absence of essence in the sense that it is the absence of essence which is the Absolute; in other words its essence is non-conceptual. The essence of the non-conceptual Wisdom Mind cannot be grasped by the conceptual mind and so, from the point of view of the conceptual mind, it is without essence; from its own point of view it is Absolute Reality.

Non-Conceptual Jnana

Thus, according to the Shentong interpretation, the *Ratnagotravibhaga, Mahayanasutralamkara* and *Madhyantavibhaga* all teach in different terms that the mind's true nature is the non-conceptual Wisdom Mind and that this is the ultimate Absolute Reality.

As long as this is not realized the Clear Light Nature acts as the basis for the impure, mistaken or illusory appearances to manifest. In other words it is the basis for the manifestation of samsara. Once it is realized, it is the basis for pure manifestations, in other words the Buddha *Kayas* (bodies) and Buddha Realms, the Mandalas of Tantric Deities and so on.

The Wisdom Mind is both emptiness and luminosity at the same time. The emptiness expresses its non-conceptual nature and the luminosity expresses its power to manifest the impure and pure appearances.

This is the view that links the sutras and the tantras. It is taught in the sutras of the third Wheel of the Doctrine and is the basis for all the tantric practices. The latter should be seen as special means for speeding up the realization process. In terms of the view, it is the same as that found in the sutras

Dream Example

When the dream was used as an example in the explanation of the other views, the emphasis was very much on the illusory nature of the dream appearances. From the Shentong point of view the comparison goes even further than this, because dreams quite clearly arise from the luminous quality of the mind itself. The mind itself can produce good and bad dreams and can continue a dream even after it has become aware that it is dreaming. Thus they can manifest whether the mind is unaware or aware. In the same way the Clear Light Nature of Mind is the basis for both samsara, which is when the mind is unaware of its own nature, and nirvana, which is when the mind is aware of its own nature.

Whether the mind is aware or unaware of its own nature, that nature does not change. It is always empty of the imaginary and dependent natures. However, as long as the non-conceptual, non-arising Wisdom Mind is not recognized, the dependent nature seems to arise, creating the dream manifestations that the confused mind imagines to comprise an outer world interacting with inner minds. From this confusion the idea of self and other, attachment and aversion, and all the other concepts and afflictions (*klesha*) that cause us suffering arise. It is just like getting totally confused and involved in a dream. Once the awakened consciousness returns, however, one quickly sees the dreams as merely manifestations of the play of the mind, and whether they subside immediately or not, they do not disturb the mind at all.

Method of Investigation

The key to this method of meditation (or rather non-meditation) is held by those who have the realization themselves. Finally there is no substitute for personal instruction from a realized master who can, through his own skill-in-means on the one hand, and the faith and devotion of the disciple on the other, cause the realization to arise and mature in the disciple's mind.

However, much can be done to prepare the mind and that is what this meditation progression on Emptiness is designed to do. By carefully practising each stage in the meditation progression until some real experience of each level of realization has arisen in the mind, one's understanding deepens and the conceptualizing tendency loses its tight hold on the mind.

Gradually the mind becomes more relaxed and open. Doubts and hesitations lose their strength and begin to disappear. The mind is naturally more calm and clear. Such a mind is more likely to respond readily and properly to the teacher's oral instructions.

In Kongtrul's *Encyclopaedia of Knowledge*, he says that the Rangtong is the view for when one is establishing certainty through listening, studying and reflecting. Shentong is the view for meditation practice.

Meditation Procedure

By the time one comes to meditation based on the Clear Light Nature of the Mind, the investigation stage of the practice has come to an end. All there is to do now is to rest the mind naturally in its own nature, just as it is without any contrivance or effort. As Jamgon Kongtrul says in the section on *shamatha* and *vipashyana* in his *Encyclopaedia of Knowledge*, whatever thoughts arise, there is no need to try to stop them; in that state they simply liberate themselves. It is like waves on an ocean that simply come to rest by themselves. No effort is required to still them.

Meditation can be done, as before, in sessions beginning with taking Refuge and arousing *Bodhichitta*, followed by dedication for the benefit of all beings. It can also be continued between sessions. From time to time one can stop what one is doing and rest the mind in its Clear Light Nature, and then try to carry that awareness over into whatever one is doing.

Generally speaking, however, when one first starts to meditate on the Clear Light Nature of Mind in the Shentong way, one's mind is far from being free of conceptual effort. Sometimes there will be the effort to see the emptiness of what arises, sometimes the effort to see the Clear Light Nature, sometimes the effort to see them both as inseparable, sometimes the effort to grasp the non-conceptual state, to understand it intellectually or to try to fix and maintain it somehow. Thus in the early stages one's meditation will not be a lot different from the early stages of the Chittamatra. This does not matter, since this is moving in the right direction. Knowing the different ways of meditating helps one to recognize the level of realization that one is approaching. Knowing the subtle faults of that level of realization helps one to overcome them.

Conclusion

Dharma consists of view, meditation and action. In this meditation progression on Emptiness we first establish the view in a simple and brief form. This is important because if the view is wrong, the meditation will be also.

Following on from having established what is the right view, comes the actual meditation. Meditation (*sgom* in Tibetan) means to train by accustoming oneself. This requires discipline and perseverance in the practice until realization arises.

Finally, following on from the meditation comes the conduct that accords with the meditation. The meditation causes one's mind and attitude to change and this means a change in one's conduct.

This meditation progression on Emptiness needs to be carefully examined with the critical mind that is searching for the true and precise nature of reality. The Buddha said that we should not just accept his words out of respect for him, or for any other reason. We should examine them for ourselves to see if they are true or not. Only if we find them true and conducive to the good and wholesome should we accept them. We should examine the teachings like a merchant buying gold. He tests the gold by means of one test after another until he is perfectly sure it is pure and flawless. Only then does he accept it. In the same way we should examine the teachings until we are sure they are true and without fault. Only then should we accept them.

Explanation of Some Key Terms

The range of the Buddha's teachings is organized in a number of ways. There are the three Vehicles (*Yana*), numerous schools and three Turnings of the Wheel of the Dharma (*Dharmachakra*).

The Three Vehicles

These are the Hinayana (comprised of Pratyekabuddhayana and Shravakayana), Mahayana and Vajrayana. This division is stressed in Tibetan Buddhism which calls itself Three Yana Buddhism. Three Yana Buddhism originated in India and is taught in all Tibetan Buddhist schools.

Dharmachakras

According to Mahayana literature, each sutra spoken by the Buddha is associated with a certain *Dharmachakra*. In the sutras it is taught that the Buddha turned the Wheel of the Dharma three times. The first time he taught that *dharmas* exist but that they are not the self. The second time he taught that *dharmas* do not exist. They are empty. The third time he taught that Absolute Reality is the Clear Light Nature of the Mind.

Although Vajrayana corresponds to the view of the third *Dharmachakra*, it is based on the Tantras rather than the Sutra tradition. Thus Vajrayana in not included in the three *Dharmachakras*.

In this *Progressive Stages of Meditation on Emptiness* the Shravaka not-self stage represents the Hinayana view of the first *Dharmachakra*. The Madhyamaka Rangtong (Svatantrika and Prasangika) represents the Mahayana view of the second *Dharmachakra*.

Shentong represents the Mahayana view of the third *Dharmachakra* which is further developed in Vajrayana.

Khenpo Tsultrim often divides the Buddha's teaching into four;

1. The way things appear to exist e.g. rebirth, karma cause and effect, atoms and moments of consciousness. This corresponds to the first *Dharmachakra*.

2. The way all things are fundamentally mind. In other words there is no difference in substance between mind and matter. This is the doctrine of the Chittamatra.

3. The way things really are. In other words, empty of true existence. This is the doctrine of the sutras of the second *Dharmachakra*.

4. The ultimate reality of the way things really are. In other words things manifest as the play of the Clear Light Nature of Mind. This doctrine is found in the sutras of the *third Dharmachakra*, in Shentong and in Vajrayana.

Buddhist Schools

Many schools of Buddhism sprang up in India and the countries to which Buddhism spread. Certain formulations of the Buddha's doctrine are associated with each school. The diagram below shows the relationship between some of the main philosophical schools that originated in India.

Translator's Notes in Regard to 2016 Edition

Throughout the text where Rinpoche said *rtag gcig rang dbang can* in Tibetan, in this edition I have translated the phrase as permanent, single and independent.

In earlier editions I translated *rtag* as 'lasting'. Permanent is more accurate. In the earlier editions *gcig* was usually translated as 'separate'. The Tibetan is simply the word for 'one'. The question is whether it should be translated as one, single or unitary? Or are they all equally good translations? I leave readers to judge for themselves. Why was 'separate' used in the earlier editions? It was a mistake. Separate is closer in meaning to 'independent' than to 'one'. So 'one' has to be mentioned too. It means 'one' in the sense of unitary or indivisible.

Wherever I have included Tibetan or Sanskrit in italics, I have left the Sanskrit without diacritics and spelt in such a way that any reader can pronounce it more or less correctly. For example I write 'ch' instead of 'c' for *chitta* and so on. I have mostly given the Tibetan in Wylie, which is often not pronounceable unless you know that system.

A word needs to be added in regard to the Tibetan terms, rangtong, Rangtongpas. Rangtong literally means 'self-empty' and is a term coined in Tibet (it does not occur in Sanskrit) to distinguish 'emptiness' when applied to conditioned phenomena (*dharmas*) that are illusory from 'Emptiness' when applied to the Non-conditioned, which is not illusory. It is empty of conditioned *dharmas* - in other words, empty of everything other than itself. It is therefore referred to as Shentong, which literally means 'Empty-of-other'. Since it refers to the Non-conditioned I have used a capital letter for it. It is synonymous with Wisdom Mind (*Jnana/Yeshe*), Buddha Nature and Absolute Reality, *Bodhichitta* and so on.

A Shentongpa is a person who accepts that the Buddha taught both the self-emptiness of the conditioned *dharmas* and the Emptiness-of-other of the Wisdom Mind.

A Rangtongpa is a person who accepts that the Buddha taught only the self-emptiness of the *dharmas*.

It is not the case that a Shentongpa rejects rangtong. There is no realisation of Shentong without a realisation of rangtong. Rangtongpas on the other hand might well reject Shentong. Some teachers call themselves Rangtongpas because rangtong is what they teach. It is not necessarily that they reject Shentong. It might simply be that they don't use that term.

Where Emptiness is used in the Shentong sense of the Absolute empty of what is other than itself, I have spelt it with a capital letter as I have all terms for the Absolute. Where it is used in the rangtong sense of the emptiness of conditioned *dharmas* I have spelt it with lower case. Where emptiness is used as a general reference to emptiness including both rangtong and Shentong, whether a capital letter is used or not depends on the context.

The Translator

Lama Shenpen Hookham had already studied and practised in retreat in India and Nepal under the direction of Kagyu Lamas for ten years before meeting Khenpo Tsultrim Gyamtso Rinpoche in 1977. She first met Trungpa Rinpoche in 1967 and followed his suggestion to go to India to take meditation instruction from Karma Thinley Rinpoche. When Karma Thinley Rinpoche left for Canada, she studied with Kalu Rinpoche and Bokar Rinpoche until in 1975 HH Karmapa asked her to return to the West to teach. She acted as Gendun Rinpoche's translator in France for a number of years until Khenpo Rinpoche directed her to take her place at Oxford University where, in 1986, she completed her doctoral thesis on *Tathagatagarbha* doctrine according to the Shentong interpretation of the *Ratnagotravibhaga*, published under the title of 'The Buddha Within' by SUNY 1991.

She married Michael Hookham (now known as Rigdzin Shikpo) in 1982. Khenpo Rinpoche encouraged Lama Shenpen to establish the Awakened Heart Sangha and take charge of students as their Lama. This is now a worldwide spiritual community based in the UK.

She spends most of her time in semi-retreat and training her students. For more information about Lama Shenpen and her teaching activity see www.ahs.org.uk.

Made in the USA
Middletown, DE
13 September 2018